Yoyogi National
Gymnasium
and KENZO TANGE

Saikaku Toyokawa

# Yoyogi Nationa

# Gymnasium

# and

# KENZO TANGE

gi National

nasium

ZO TANGE

# Introduction:
## From a Symbol of an Era of Growth
## to a Symbol of an Era of Maturity


On October 19, 1964, President Brundage of the International Olympic Committee (IOC) presented the Olympic Diploma of Merit to the architect who designed Yoyogi National Gymnasium, Kenzo Tange. Originally, the Olympic Diploma of Merit was awarded to celebrate individuals who had made special contributions to promote the Olympic Movement, but on this occasion, the award lauded the design of Tange's world-class indoor pool. Newspapers shared the IOC's comments that Kenzo Tange's work had been inspired by sports, and as evidenced by the numerous world records set in his pool, the athletes had been inspired by Tange's architecture. He had shown the tightly knit kinship between sports and the arts.

Approximately half a century later in September 2012, the IOC session assembled in Buenos Aires, designating Tokyo the host of the

2020 Olympics. The Yoyogi National Gymnasium was appointed the handball venue as the Legacy Stadium of the Heritage Zone.

For those from the generation accustomed to the time of high economic growth in Japan, the Yoyogi National Gymnasium was a stunning achievement of the era of growth. Further, for younger generations who gather here to participate in women's fashion events, the 1st gymnasium runway is where celebreties and models show their beauty. Examining the Yoyogi gymnasium froma a broader standpoint, however, reminds us of the history of land, once used an army parade ground, then requisitioned by GHQ after Japan's surrender, and reborn as a gymnasium in service of the Olympic Charter's goal to "[build] a peaceful and better world." With an appearance unchanged from the time of its completion, the Yoyogi National Gymnasium is intended as a sanctum for sports, preserved to this day as an exemplary theater of entertainment fit for the times. Yoyogi could be said to be a condensed chronicle of 20th century Japan, and the dauntless Yoyogi National Gymnasium a cultural heritage of the same era. In radical terms, the Yoyogi National Gymnasium has been sublimated from a symbol of an epoch of era to one of maturity.

Chapter 1 of this text, "Architectural Works of Kenzo Tange: 5 Characteristics," reviews the career of the architect responsible for Yoyogi National Gymnasium, Kenzo Tange, and examines the elements required to analyze the gymnasium's essence as well as to clarify the characteristics of Tange's design.

Chapter 2, titled "Yoyogi National Gymnasium Understood through Urban Design," charts the many changes the urban plan and Yoyogi environs underwent during the Meiji, Taisei, early Showa, and postwar years, retracing its time as a pre-war army parade ground to the postwar Washington Heights, as well as the process of its return to Japan just before the Olympics.

Chapter 3, titled "Yoyogi National Gymnasium Understood through Architectural Design," follows in detail (with the aid of primary source materials) the processes of selecting the designing architect, drafting the preliminary and working designs, and building on the construction site.

Chapter 4, titled "Yoyogi National Gymnasium After the Tokyo Olympics," lays out the measures taken by the organization responsible for managing and maintaining the facility since its completion, the National Gymnasium Special Public Institution (known today as the Japan Sport Council).

Lastly, the author is well aware of the skepticism of the necessity for and criticisms of holding the Tokyo Olympics and Paralympics in 2020 in this era of maturity and whether its bid contributed to the reconstruction from the Great East Japan Earthquake. There is no question that these topics contain numerous points worth heeding. Even so, regardless of the answers to these two points, the author of this book hopes to expound here on the Yoyogi National Gymnasium's identity as a legacy of the Olympics, for the role it has served in the history of 20th century Japan and for its architectural beauty.

# Contents

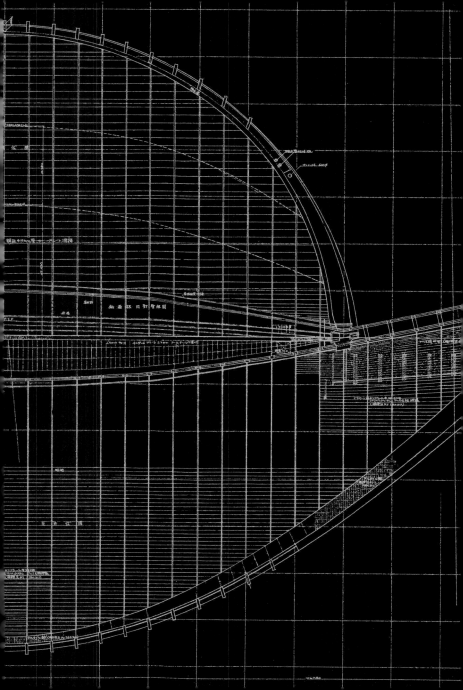

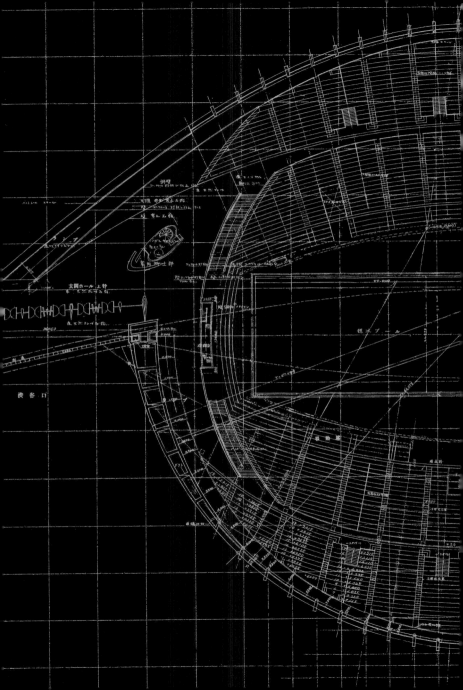

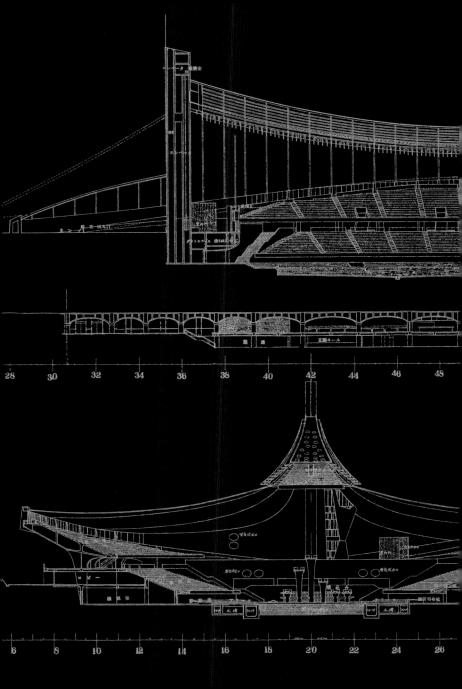

エレベーター機械室

室内

エレベーター

スロープ屋体出入口

浴室

玄関ホール

| | | | | | | | | | | |
|28|30|32|34|36|38|40|42|44|46|48|

非常脱出口

割出口

非常脱出口

ロビー

機械室

競技司令室

天達 |500| |500| 土達

| | | | | | | | | | | |
|6|8|10|12|14|16|18|20|22|24|26|

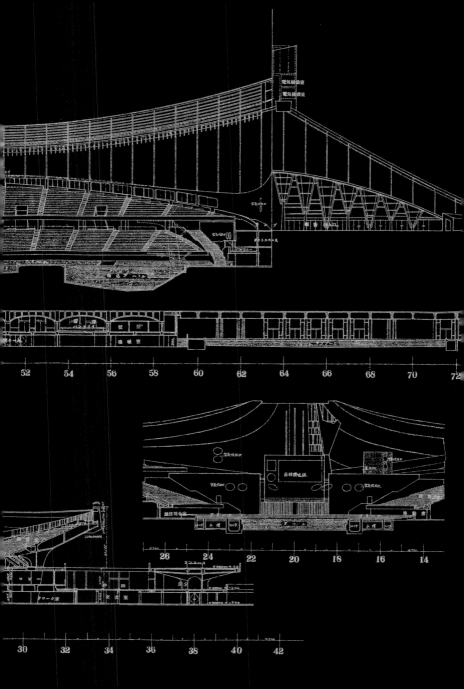

電気機械室
電気機械室

空気吹込口

ポートスペース

52  54  56  58  60  62  64  66  68  70  72

空気吹出口  排気吹出口
女子便所
空気吹込口  空気吹出口
競技司令室  審判席
水槽  水槽

26  24  22  20  18  16  14

ロック室  更衣室

30  32  34  36  38  40  42

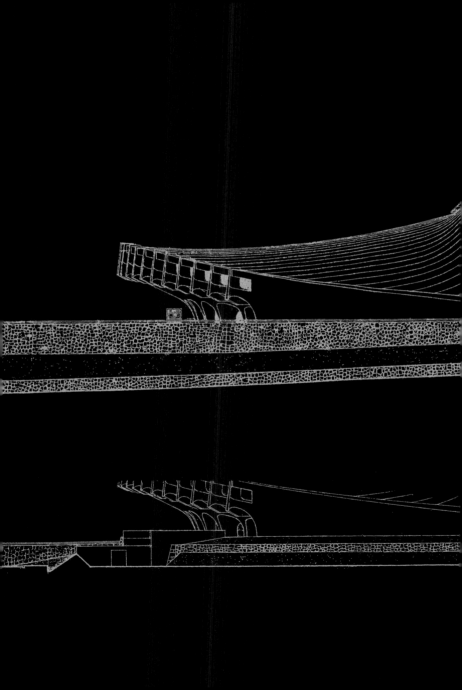

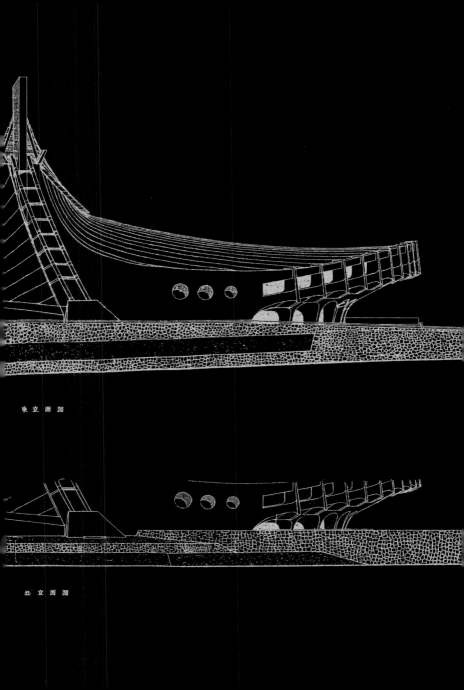

東 立 面 図

西 立 面 図

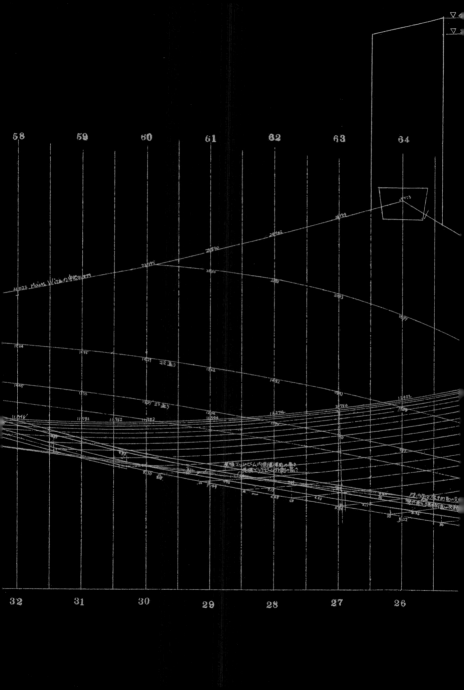

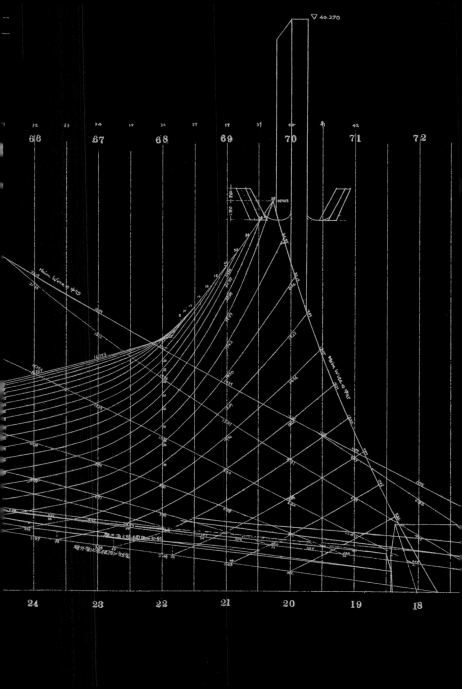

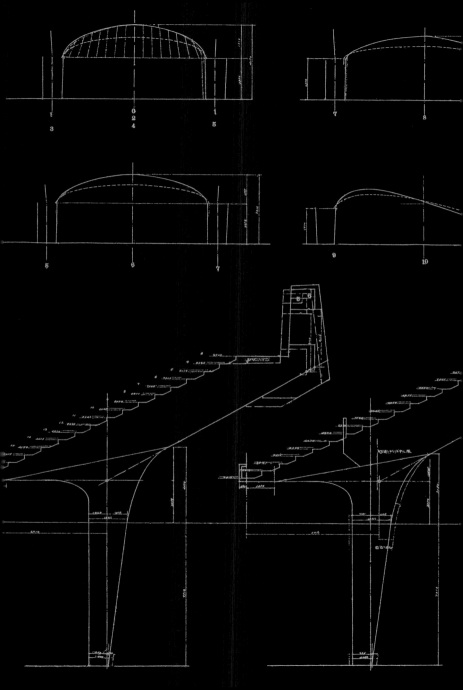

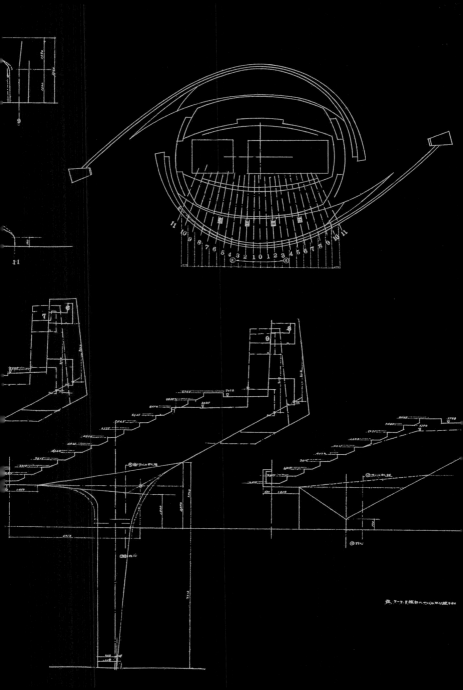

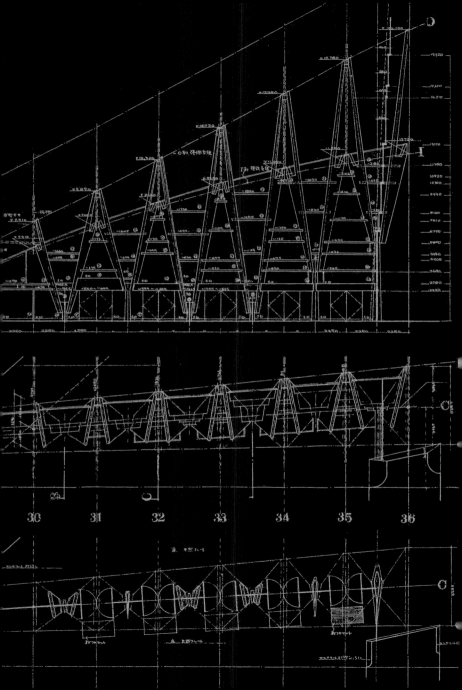

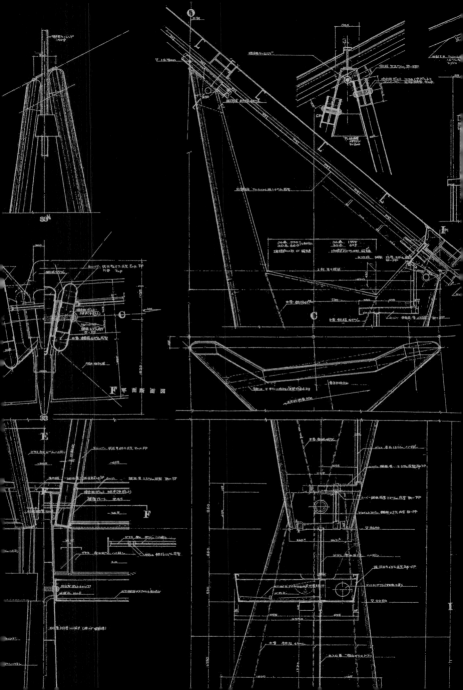

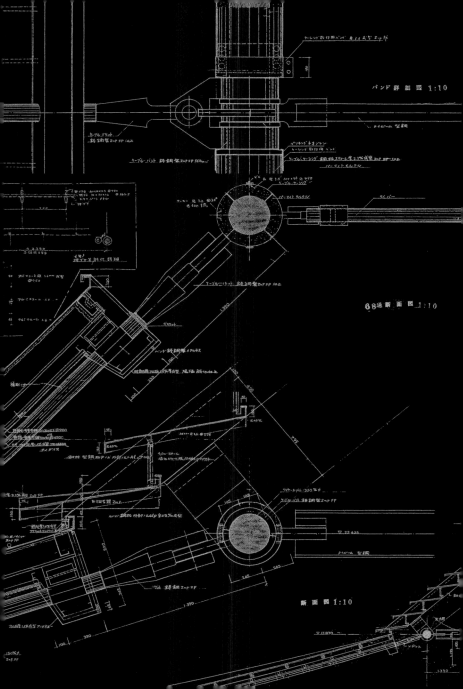

バンド詳細図 1:10

68通断面図 1:10

断面図 1:10

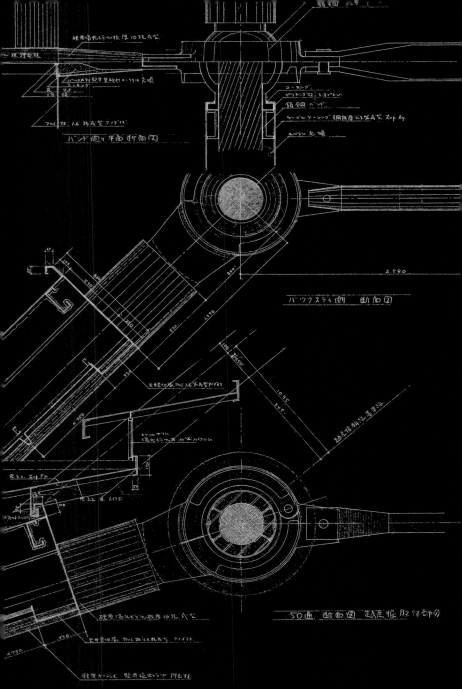

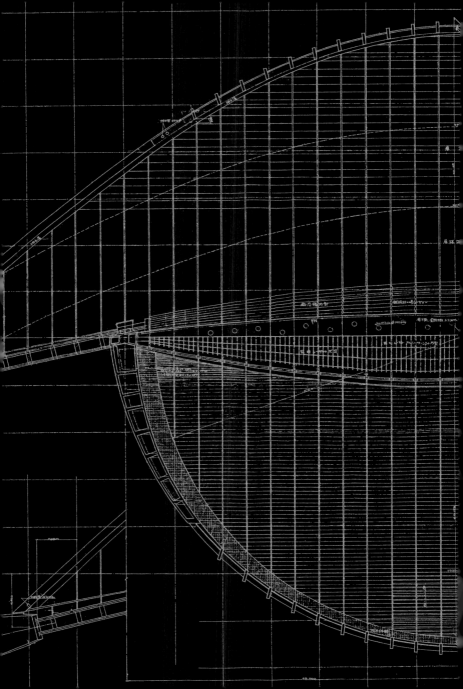

# Yoyogi Nationa

# Gymnasium

# and

# KENZO TANGE

# 1

# Architectural Works of Kenzo Tange: 5 Characteristics

# 1-1

## Modern vs. Traditional Architecture: Tange's Philosophy of Deconstruction and Reconstruction

Born in Osaka in 1913, Kenzo Tange enrolled in the Department of Architecture at Tokyo Imperial University. The Modern Movement of architecture in Europe was introduced to Japan in the late 1920s, and architectural students at the time were fascinated by the white box modern architecture presented. Meanwhile, Tange was engrossed in the Palace of the Soviets by Le Corbusier, whom he rated highly and considered of all architects a genius. As a result, Tange proposed a public building strongly influenced by Le Corbusier in his graduation design project, Art House *[fig.1-1]*.

When Tange graduated from Tokyo Imperial University's Department of Architecture in 1938, Tokyo Teishin Hospital (designed by Mamoru Yamada) was completed, and a myriad of young architects and students were enthralled by its stylish exterior. But Tange surprised his fellow students by stating that the building was as clean as sanitary ware but not emotionally moving.

[fig.1-1] *Kenzo Tange graduation design project perspective drawing*

What separated Le Corbusier's architecture from Tokyo Teishin Hospital? At that time, architecture stripped of traditional decoration in pursuit of rationality and functionality was highly acclaimed, and white boxes with necessary holes opened on the sides attracted the attention of young architects. Tange was not emotionally moved by such white boxes. He declared that architecture without the ability to touch one's heart is incomplete and stated that Le Corbusier's architecture alone was an example which did have this ability. Tange discovered a structure analogous to the relationship between pre-modern and modern architecture, in 16th century Italy, a long distance both in time and place from 20th century Japan. He overlapped the occurrence of modern architecture with the emergence of Renaissance architecture emphasizing geometry from the heavily decorated Gothic architecture. Of all Renaissance architecture, Tange vigorously praised Michelangelo's as magnificent and exceptional. It can be said that he rejected the existing interpretation and recognition towards common architecture and sought the fundamental character of architecture in the works of Le Corbusier and Michelangelo. Young Tange continued to hold such views even after the war, and was deeply impressed by Michelangelo's Capitoline Hill and Farnese Palace when he visited Rome on his first overseas business trip in 1951 *[fig.1-2, 1-3]*. Tange was moved by how Michelangelo and ancient Ro-

[fig.1-2] Postcard of Capitoline Hill
Tange sent from Rome

[fig.1-3] Farnese Palace
(exterior by Michelangelo)

[fig.1-4] Hiroshima Peace Memorial Park

man architecture were designed on a divine scale compared to modern architecture designed to the human scale in accordance with physical human dimensions, and wished that his designs would be like Michelangelo's [fig.1-4].

On the other hand, many modern architects visited Japan in the 1930s–1950s, praising classic Japanese architecture. For example, German architect Bruno Taut applauded the Katsura Imperial Villa while he criticized the ornamented Nikko Toshogu Shrine. Similarly, Taut called Ise Jingu the Parthenon of the East, delighting many Japanese architects. When Harvard Graduate School of Design faculty member Walter Gropius visited Japan in 1954 [fig.1-5], he praised traditional Japanese homes as having all the indicators of modern architecture. For instance, Japanese homes are spatially open,

[fig.1-5] Gropius visiting Kurashiki (1954)

which is consistent with modern architecture's notion of continuous spaces. The standard approaches to tatami (a type of flooring), fusuma (papered partitions), and shoji (papered sliding doors) coincide with modular coordination essential for industrial products. Movable partitions realized by tatami and fusuma shares the notions of flexible spaces which modern architecture seeks. Traditional Japanese architecture has been supported by craftsmanship, and even in the case of modern architecture, the balance between crafts and automation is still important. The Zen spirit and modern architectural principles are similar; the rock garden of Ryoanji which expresses Oriental spirituality harbors ideals close to that of modern architecture.

A book commemorating Gropius's visit was set to be published in Japan after his return to the United States. To this book, Tange submitted an essay in which he both vehemently opposed and agreed to Gropius's concise evaluation of Japanese architecture. He writes that although the actual sight of Katsura Imperial Villa and its eye-catching decorations did not impress him at all, the beautiful proportionality inherent in the Villa would grow inside his heart on recollection of the Villa after returning home and would stimulate his creativity *[fig.1-6]*. When Tange later met photographer Yasuhiro Ishimoto, he was astonished at how Ishimoto's photographs captured Katsura Imperial Villa

*[fig.1-6] Tange taking photographs at Katsura Imperial Villa (1955)*

from a new perspective. Ishimoto studied architectural photography in Chicago and photographed Katsura Imperial Villa in the 1950s; with adept photo cropping techniques, he succeeded in drawing out the horizontal and vertical geometry concealed in the villa *[fig.1-7]*. Tange praised the abilities of the yet young Ishimoto and in 1960 produced the publication of his photography book Katsura (MIT Press). In this book co-authored by Tange and Gropius, Tange asserts in the beginning that his viewpoint differs from those that regard Katsura as the crystallization of an elegant world, declaring that his view of Katsura is destructive.

In this way, on the one hand Tange pursued the fundamental character of architecture in Le Corbusier and Michelangelo while criticizing the well-regarded Teishin Hospital, and on the other destructively perceived

*[fig.1-7] Trimmed camber on the Katsura Imperial Villa exterior (1955)*

the outsider and elitist evaluation of Katsura Imperial Villa by Taut and Gropius by borrowing Ishimoto's angles. Tange throughout the 1950s rejected popular notions of architecture from all eras and regions, overcame the boundaries of modern and traditional styles, and himself deconstructed and reconstructed his own style of architectural analysis.

# 1-2
## War and Peace:
## Creation of Memorial Spaces

After graduation, Tange went to work at the architectural design firm of Le Corbusier's disciple Kunio Mayekawa, before returning to Tokyo Imperial University for graduate school. During World War II, he worked at Hongo Campus of the Tokyo Imperial University conducting research and design on urban planning and architecture. During this time, Tange entered and won first place in a competition sponsored by the Architectural Institute of Japan for the design of the Greater East Asia Co-Prosperity Sphere Memorial Hall *[fig.1-8]*. The design proposal was intended for a facility situated at the foot of Mt. Fuji commemorating students sent off to and killed in the war (student soldiers). To this end, Tange first constructed a long axis (a highway) from Tokyo's imperial palace to Mt. Fuji, and

*[fig.1-8] Greater East Asia Co-Prosperity Sphere Memorial Hall plan*

then on either side placed two vast trapezoidal shaped plazas at the foot of the mountain. The method of dynamically placing together two trapezoids to compose a plaza was similar to what Le Corbusier had prepared for the Palace of the Soviets. By setting a 60m tall main hall designed with an enormous roof modeled after that of Ise Jingu in the trapezoidal plaza, Tange planned to integrate a Japanese-style roof with a Western European plaza. Further, in the 1944 competition held for the Japanese–Thai cultural center in Bangkok, Tange won first place by submitting a plan that arranged several buildings with grand roofs imitating Ise Jingu's, similar to his plan for the Greater East Asia Co-Prosperity Sphere Memorial Hall.

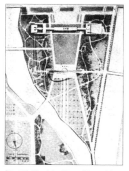

[fig.1-9] Hiroshima Peace Memorial Park and Museum design competition site plan, first proposal

Tange became an assistant professor at the architectural department of Tokyo Imperial University in the postwar years. In 1949 he won first place in the design competition for the Hiroshima Peace Memorial Park and Museum. In the plan he proposed the following in his design. From the Atomic Bomb Dome, situated across the river on the north side of the site (Nakajima Park), an axis was drawn south; in the center of the site a green plaza where 50,000 city residents could gather was placed; and on the south side of the site, the public hall (west), a museum (center), and a main building (east) were placed along a straight line from west to east [fig.1-9, 1-10]. Newspapers published word of the Atomic Bomb Dome's demolition at the time of the competition, but

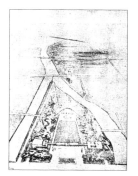

[fig.1-10] Hiroshima Peace Memorial Park and Museum design competition perspective drawing, first proposal

Tange believed that the dome should be preserved as an eternal reminder of the atomic bomb's cruelty and inhumanity. Further, Tange designed the site plan so that by viewing the Atomic Bomb Dome with the pilotis-supported museum in the foreground, people who had gathered to renew their hopes for peace on one riverbank (shigan, or this world) would face the Atomic Bomb Dome on the other (higan, or otherworld). Although this plan won first prize, numerous complications twisted its path to completion such that it was only finished just before the bombing anniversary on August 6, 1955. Hiroshima's mayor, Shinzo Hamai, read a moving declaration of peace and Tange himself participated in the ceremony.[1]

Examining the Hiroshima Peace Memorial Park facilities offers insights into the unique relationship between Tange's treatment of materials and view of architectural history. For example, Tange built his own residence in suburban Tokyo's Seijo area in 1952. He is considered to have conducted research on the thin proportion of Katsura Imperial Villa through the design of this two-storied wooden structure supported on pilotis. Meanwhile, when designing the Hiroshima Peace Memorial Park's main building and museum, Tange completed the former by applying the thin proportions of Katsura Imperial Villa to concrete architecture, but realized the latter by strongly evoking Ise Jingu's dynamic design [fig. 1-11, 1-12].

[fig.1-11] Hiroshima Peace Memorial Park main building, museum (1954)

34

Similarities between Tange's and Le Corbusier's architecture can be identified in the Hiroshima Peace Memorial Park Design, where the museum's pilotis strongly resembles the lower section of Le Corbusier's Unité d'Habitation. It is probable that Tange discovered and applied what he found inspiring from traditional Japanese architecture and Le Corbusier's latest work. Tange also emulated Le Corbusier's use of the Modulor concept (a dimensional system based on the Fibonacci sequence) with the preparation of his own Tange Modulor, determining design according to these sequences. It may be said that while Le Corbusier's Modulor was aimed at harmonizing physical human dimensions and architecture, Tange sought to use his own Modulor to control the entire urban plan including architecture.

Approximately ten years after the com-

[fig.1-12] Hiroshima Peace Memorial
Park main building exterior (1955)

pletion of Hiroshima Peace Memorial Park, at the request of the Relief Association for

the Mobilized Students, Tange designed a plaza for student soldiers and mobilized youth at the summit of Awaji-shima to commemorate those sent off to war never to return. Tange maintained his principle of designing

[fig.1-13] Memorial Plaza for Students Who Perished in the War, tower, long shot (left)

[fig.1-14] Memorial Plaza for Students Who Perished in the War, tower, close low angle shot (right)

an axis as he had in other memorial spaces, and here designed a 25m tall tower representing a link between heaven and earth, using an HP (hyperbolic paraboloid) shell to draw the gazes of visitors [fig. 1-13–15].[2]

[fig.1-15] Memorial Plaza for Students Who Perished in the War, interior

# 1-3
# Postwar Democracy and
# Design of Government Buildings

In 1945, many of Japan's cities had been reduced to ashes by US air raids, and Tokyo was no exception. Tange began work on designing government buildings suited for postwar democracy, and in 1957 completed the Tokyo Metropolitan Government Office (hereafter referred to as the former Tokyo Metropolitan Government Office) in Yurakucho (current site of the Tokyo International Forum). The current Tokyo Metropolitan Government Office, also designed by Tange, is located in Shinjuku.

When designing the former Tokyo Metropolitan Government Office, Tange paid particular attention to the urban overpopulation, as well as the reduction of thermal load and noise pollution. He selected the core system and pilotis to resolve the former. A core system is a method often employed in typical office buildings, where common areas (i.e., elevators, stairwells, restrooms, and utility pipes) are concentrated at the center of the structure's floor plan, and surrounded by seismic walls and dedicated spaces (universal spaces). Tange expected many workers to commute to Yurakucho at the center of Tokyo and overcrowd the central facility, the former Tokyo Metropolitan Government Office. His design philosophy was to gather the many commuting workers in the wide-open public space comprised from a pilotis, quickly sort and send them to their designated floors by elevator or stairs, such that the pilotis would be free from congestion and would serve as a relaxing public space where the surrounding citizens could socially interact [fig.1-16].

To address the latter (reduction in thermal load and noise pollution), Tange proposed employing eaves, louvers, and fins. According to calculations conducted at the time of the competition, Tange estimated that these architectural elements would reduce the winter thermal load to that of a building with a 50% window to wall ratio and cut summer thermal load by 90% such that the cost of the elements would be depreciated in approximately 5 years. He also emphasized the usefulness of eaves, louvers, and fins in supplying a homogeneous illuminance distribution as wells as the functionality of eaves in allowing opening of windows in comfortable climate conditions [fig.1-17, 1-18]. Regarding the noise pollution, it was required to reduce the 80dB noise level to the applicable limit of 40dB. Since empirical data regarding

*[fig.1-16] Urban core and architectural core of the former Tokyo Metropolitan Government Office*

*Trains and automobiles move horizontally from all parts of the metropolitan area toward the government office (urban core).*

*Elevators (architectural core) of the government office move vertically to disperse the flow of people into each floor.*

*Pilotis at the foot of the government office is a pleasant space with less passers-by except during rush hours.*

*[fig.1-17] Former Tokyo Metropolitan Government Office exterior*

[fig.1-18] Ceramic mural
by Taro Okamoto installed in the pilotis
of the former Tokyo Metropolitan
Government Office

Architectural Works of Kenzo Tange: 5 Characteristics

noise reduction was lacking at the time, Tange hoped that the proper selection of materials for the eaves, louvers, and fins would provide some sound insulation.

When the former Tokyo Metropolitan Government Office was completed, however, the number of metropolitan officials had doubled from what the building capacity had been designed for, suddenly reducing the facility's usability. Further, Japan at the time lacked the technology to produce stainless steel louvers and sashes, and bending and installation of thin steel plates resulted in widespread rust. On this point, Tange states with regret, "An architect loses possession of an architectural design the minute it's completed, and in this way it's like giving away your daughter at a wedding. They've been kind enough to contin-

[fig.1-19] Kagawa Prefectural
Government Office exterior

ue using the Tokyo Metropolitan Government Building for a long time despite the difficulties, but I pity my daughter."[3]

Later, Tange had the opportunity to design the likes of Kurayoshi City Hall, Imabari City Public Hall, and Kurashiki City Hall, but based on lessons learned from the former Tokyo Metropolitan Government Office, he began to aspire using concrete in government buildings. Completed in 1958, the Kagawa Prefectural Government Office in particular, crystallized Tange's mastery of government architecture. As opposed to the former Tokyo Metropolitan Government Office intended to display a metallic exterior, Tange candidly expressed the beauty of concrete in the Kagawa Prefectural Government Office. On the other hand, the balconies and eaves Tange experimented on the former Tokyo Metropolitan Government Office are employed in the Kagawa Prefectural Government Office design, and the pilotis and core system are further refined. And so the Kagawa Prefectural Government Office was realized in a perfected state as an office space and a public space for city residents [fig.1-19–22].

[fig.1-20, 1-21] *Kagawa Prefectural Government Office exterior (photograph by Tange)*

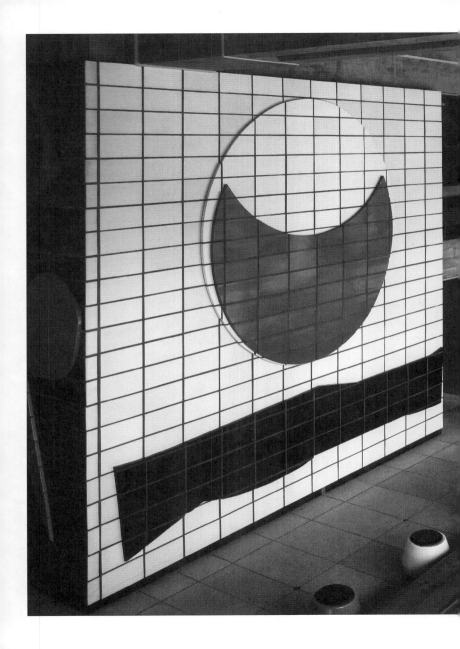

[fig.1-22] Ceramic mural
by Genichiro Inokuma installed in
the pilotis of the Kagawa Prefectural
Government Office

## 1-4
## Endeavors to
## Large Span Structures

In 1948, three years after the atomic bomb was dropped over Hiroshima, Kenzo Tange submitted a proposal for a ribbed Schalen frame (author's note: shell structure) to the Hiroshima Memorial Cathedral for World Peace competition. In the statement, Tange explains the reason behind the selection of the shell structure as follows:

> We sought in modern architecture to move the hearts of modern people, to make them feel the heightening of their spirits. So I tried to discover a new, inspiring aspect in the Schalen frame itself—in the composition of rational, economic lines.[4]

Tange points out that the shell structure, a uniquely modern technique, combines rationality and economy while bearing the potential to stir viewers at a spiritual level. The judges selected Tange for second prize with no one for first, which lead to Togo Murano, who was one of the judges, to take on the role of the designer.

It was the structural engineer Yoshikatsu Tsuboi (of Tokyo Imperial University's Second Faculty of Engineering, currently the Institute of Industrial Science at the University of Tokyo) who brought Tange's vision for shell construction to fruition. In 1950, Tange won the Hiroshima Peace Memorial

Park competition and received a request from the city to design a children's lirary north of the park on the shores of the river Ota-gawa. Tange initially considered an ordinary, circular library with two stories, but he took Tsuboi's advice and designed a circular, bell-shaped shell structure 20m across, which was completed in 1952 *[fig.1-23]*.

*[fig.1-23] Hiroshima Children's Library exterior*

In the following year in 1953, Tange and Tsuboi together completed the Ehime Prefectural Hall. Built for the National Sports Festival, the building had a 50m span domed shell structure (a portion of a sphere was cut out on a plane). Though the Ehime Prefectural Hall was originally intended as a sports facility, it was often used to hold concerts since Matsuyama at the time lacked sufficient indoor facilities to house large audiences. In order to solve the acoustical problems, sound-absorbing devices were later installed in the hall *[fig.1-24]*.

*[fig.1-24] Ehime Prefectural Hall exterior*

In 1957, Tange and Tsuboi completed the former Shizuoka Convention Hall which had a square floor plan. The roof of this gymnasium consisted of a reinforced concrete HP shell with 54m on each side (shaped like a handkerchief held at two ends with the other two pressed to the ground). Although Tange hoped in the design phase to support the enormous roof with just two pillars and no walls, a long ribbed wall extending to the roof's edges was constructed on all four sides of the hall. Tange recalled later that the long ribbed wall and shell structure were not sufficiently unified in the design.[5] After the Shizuoka Convention Hall's completion, however, several concrete fragments of the shell structure fell. Fortunately the accident injured no one. Some of the causes for the failure are considered to be the following: excessive deformation of the pipes supporting the shell formwork due to the large number of workers hauling in ready-made concrete in wheelbarrows at once in order to follow an extremely tight construction schedule, poorly cast shell concrete due to rain, deformation due to heat shrinkage, and inherent fragility of the HP shell which must support both tension and compression [fig.1-25].[6]

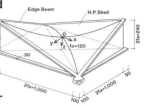

[fig.1-25] Shizuoka Convention Hall, an illustration before making a model of HP shell

In the 1960s, Tange and Tsuboi concurrently designed the Yoyogi National Gymnasium and Saint Mary's Cathedral, Tokyo. Regarding the cathedral, eight HP shells are structured to overlap and support each other [fig.1-26]. Tange points out three key aspects to the cathedral's design. First, the main part of the cathedral consisting of the HP shell structured vertically symbolizes the Catholic spirit in form, just like how

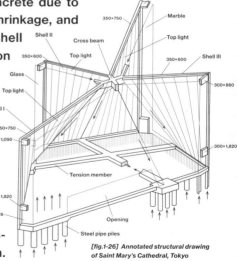

[fig.1-26] Annotated structural drawing of Saint Mary's Cathedral, Tokyo the medieval temple served as a symbol of the community and asserts its verticality within the city skyline. The slopes of the HP shells are rounded to blend in with the Japanese urban environment. Second, the psychological change that occurs in the visitors entering the church is taken into consideration such that they do not directly enter the church from the busy street but gradually approach it in the order of busy street, small plaza, plaza hidden from the street, and finally the church. Third, a transcendental world is constructed within the cathedral interior through concrete technology, since it symbolizes the microcosm of the soul. By combining the HP shell's bold vertical frame with a classical cross-shaped plan, Tange and Tsuboi invoke spiritual mystery *[fig.1-27]*.[7]

*[fig.1-27] Interior of Saint Mary's Cathedral, Tokyo*

Though Tange considered constructing the HP shell from precast concrete in the early phases of design, he later realized that the entire structure could be constructed lighter by constructing the shell from ribbed reinforced concrete on site. Moreover, by using 40m long stainless steel sheets along the exterior walls, the torsion unique to HP shells are emphasized *[fig.1-28]*. Meanwhile, the cross-shaped skylight lights the massive walls of the HP shell, successfully uniting heaven and earth to achieve a majestic yet modern cathedral.

*[fig.1-28] Exterior of Saint Mary's Cathedral, Tokyo*

# 1-5
## Designs during Japans
## High Economic Growth and
## the Osaka Expo '70

On January 1, 1961, Tange appeared on NHK (Japan's national broadcaster) and announced his Plan for Tokyo 1960. According to Tange, conventional urban planning of Tokyo was hampered by the concept of a downtown in which the working population is aimed at being placed in surrounding cities (Yokohama, Maebashi, Utsunomiya, Tsukuba, Chiba, and the like). Tange, on the other hand, approved of the population concentrating in Tokyo, and instead aimed to build a highway network over Tokyo Bay while systematically reclaiming land for further economic development. Put another way, Tange drafted a plan to promote organic development by proposing to introduce a linear structure (civic axis) in favor of a centripetal one (a radial model). Further, contrary to conventional urban planning that would

[fig.1-29] Kenzo Tange standing before the Plan for Tokyo 1960 panel strengthen one function per locale—residential, manufacturing, commercial—Plan for Tokyo 1960 focused on how to smoothly connect multiple functions and placed greater importance on seamlessly linking the varying scales of architecture and the city *[fig.1-29]*.

Examining the business districts and highway transportation comprising Plan for Tokyo 1960 reveals the radical proposals made in each. Tange's business district proposes architecture capable of three-dimensional communication, suitable for an information society, as well as architecture capable of growth. This

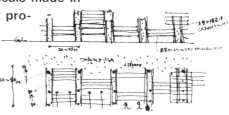

[fig.1-30] *Shizuoka central city redevelopment sketch by Arata Isozaki*

idea was realized in the Yamanashi Press and Broadcasting Center, with its 16 enormous cylindrical columns (communication shafts) housing elevators, stairwells, and utility pipes, and beams placed between these columns which allowed for selective arrangement of the floor most suitable for each function *[fig. 1-30–33]*. Put concretely, the space (area and height) required by each function such as a broadcasting station, radio station, newspaper publisher, are arranged three-dimensionally and connected organically. The facility was planned to be expanded as necessary, and continues to be used as television and radio stations and a newspaper publishing house to this day.

Next, regarding highway transportation, Plan for Tokyo 1960 proposed Cycle Transportation, a three-dimensional highway sup-

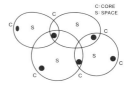

[fig.1-31] *Yamanashi Press and Broadcasting Center floor plan diagram*

[fig.1-32] *Yamanashi Press and Broadcasting Center sectional diagram*

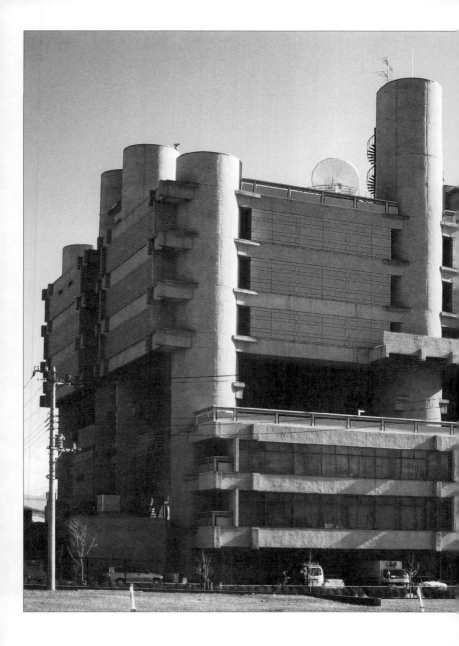

[fig.1-33] *Yamanashi Press and Broadcasting Center exterior*

porting express, medium-speed, and low-speed traffic connecting Tokyo and Kisarazu on an urban axis. Extending this idea of an urban axis to connect Tokyo and Hakata resulted in the Tokaido Megalopolis (1965). The area between Tokyo and Osaka along the Pacific Ocean (the Taiheiyo Belt) had been considered a base of postwar development, but this proposal would extend the belt in the direction of Hiroshima and Hakata while also integrating a key development zone with highway transportation. Although the shinkansen (bullet train) had begun operations between Tokyo and Osaka by 1964, and the Tomei Expressway had fully opened in 1969, it was Osaka's hosting of World Expo '70 in 1970 that established an awareness that Tokyo–Osaka was a one day business trip distance. Thus, the Tokaido Megalopolis began taking on a sense of reality.

Together with Kyoto University professor Uzo Nishiyama, Tange planned the venue for World Expo '70, considering the site as the core of a futuristic city and planned the festival plaza as a developmental model to visualize the Tokaido Megalopolis. Additionally, Waseda University professor Uichi Inouye was responsible for the festival plaza's air conditioning system and the transparent membrane roof's pressure control system [fig.1-34].

[fig.1-34] World Expo '70 festival plaza

# 1-6
## Summary

We have so far discussed five characteristics of Kenzo Tange's architectural works, which will be summarized here. First, regarding modernity and tradition, Tange rejected popular interpretations of architecture from every era and region while overcoming the boundary between modernity and tradition and deconstructing and reconstructing his own architectural analysis.

Second, regarding war and peace, Tange designed memorial spaces through Japans pre- and postwar years, ever regarding the predicament of war and peace as a crucial issue. The lining of axes to symbolic forms, the construction of plazas where people can gather, and the ingenious placement of buildings around the axes and plazas are consistent features existing in all spaces.

Third, regarding postwar democracy and design of government buildings, Tange aimed for the organic integration of the core of the city with the core architectural components, by gathering urban residents (commuters) at a building structure placed at the city center (core) and solving the problems which arise there by proper placement of architectural core components (common areas such as elevator, stairs, and plumbing). This aim is clear throughout his designs, such as in the former Tokyo Metropolitan Government Office, Kurayoshi City Hall, Kurashiki City Hall, Imabari City Public Hall, and the Kagawa Prefectural Government Office.

Fourth, regarding the endeavors to Large Span Structures, Tange's meeting with structural engineer Yoshikatsu Tsuboi enabled the realization of one shell structure after another. In their early days, Tange and Tsuboi mastered the art of shell structures through the use of bell-and cylindrical dome-shaped shells and simple geometries. This allowed them to reach the completion of Saint Mary's Cathedral, Tokyo, which skillfully employs HP shells. By building the series of shell structures, Tange and Tsuboi continued to strive for the worlds most advanced architectural design, and were able to succeed in "moving the hearts of modern people, and making them feel the heightening of their spirits."

Fifth, regarding design during Japans high economic growth and the Osaka Expo '70, Tange proposed a three-dimensional urban vision and a futuristic urban core integrated with a highway transportation system to encourage postwar Japan's rapid economic growth. With the proposal, he was able to present a point of view in which the architecture, city, and land is considered as one single megastructure. Japanese architectural and urban planning, which had mostly been limited to implementing ideas from oversea, was able to appeal itself to the world through Tange's innovative concept.

1    Kenzo Tange, "Tange kenkyu-shitsu [Tange Laboratory]," Ippon no enpitsu kara [From One Pencil] (Tokyo: Nikkei, 1985), 59.

2    Kenzo Tange, "Senbotsu gakuto wo kinen suru hiroba [A Plaza to Commemorate Fallen Student Soldiers]," Tange Kenzo: Kenchiku to Toshi [Kenzo Tange: Architecture and Cities] (Tokyo: Sekaibunka, 1975), 330.

3    Kenzo Tange, "Tange kenkyu-shitsu [Tange Laboratory]," Ippon no enpitsu kara [From One Pencil] (Tokyo: Nikkei, Inc, 1985), 66.

4    Kenzo Tange, "Hiroshima heiwa kinen Katorikku seido kenchiku kyogi sekkei setsumeisho [Hiroshima Memorial Cathedral for World Peace Architectural Competition Design Instructions]," Heiwa kinen Hiroshima Katorikku seido kenchiku kyogi sekkei sho [Hiroshima Memorial Cathedral for World Peace Architecture Competition Design Book], ed. Memorial Cathedral for World Peace (Tokyo: Koyosha, 1949), 20.

5    Kenzo Tange, "Mugen no kanosei: tetsu to konkuriito [Endless Possibilities: Iron and Concrete]," Kenchiku bunka [Architectural Culture], February, 1958.

6    "Yoshioka Miki intabyu [Miki Yoshioka Interview]," Tange Kenzo to Kenzo Tange [Tange Kenzo and Kenzo Tange], ed. Saikaku Toyokawa (Tokyo: Ohmsha, 2013), 282–283.

7    "Tokyo kyasedoraru shimei kyogi sekkei nyusen-an sekkei shushi [Tokyo Cathedral Nomination Competition Design Winning Design Overview]," Shin-kenchiku [New Architecture], July 1962, 70.

# 2

# Yoyogi National Gymnasium Understood through Urban Design

Here, we will look back on Yoyogi's history from the late modern era to present day, from three aspects of urban design (military base construction, an Olympic bid, and road construction).

# 2-1
## From the Late Modern to Late Meiji Era (late 19th century–1910s)

In the early modern era, Yoyogi, located on the outskirts of Edo, was an area where many daimyo and shogunal vassal samurai residences were located in order to defend Edo Castle. There, surrounded by swathes of agricultural land, stood the residences of the Ii clan (in the inner garden of Meiji Jingu) and the Okabe clan (in a part of today's Yoyogi National Gymnasium site) [fig.2-1].

As samurai residences and land were seized (confiscated) in the Meiji Era, what remained of the Ii clan residence came to be replaced by farmland. The residence was sold thereafter, bought by the Imperial Household Agency in 1874, and ultimately in 1889 turned into the imperial family–owned Minamitoshima District. Then in 1909, in a rural area on the south side of the imperial estate, the vast Yoyogi Parade Grounds was established.

[fig.2-1] Grade monoplane that made the first flight in Japan with Captain Kumazo Hino and Yoshitoshi Tokugawa, both a member of Temporary Military Balloon Study Group (Dec. 1, 1910, Yoyogi Parade Grounds)

Looking back at the changes in Edo/Tokyo from the standpoint of military base development, central Tokyo has seen parade ground development in Etchujima (1855–1891)[1], Hibiya (1871–1888), and Aoyama (1888–1926). With the relocation of military facilities beginning around 1887, army-related facilities were installed along the Oyama-kaido (Akasaka, Aoyama, Shibuya, Komazawa, and Mizonokuchi—now Route 246). For example, the Ministry of the Army and General Staff Office was installed at Akasaka-gomon, the starting point of Oyama-kaido; moving west, cavalry and artillery camps in addition to Aoyama Parade Grounds were installed along Oyama-kaido. Later, Komaba and Komazawa military facilities and Komazawa Parade Grounds were installed around the First Sino-Japanese War (1894–1895) and the Russo-Japanese War (1904–1905), and a major military base came to encompass the area from Akasaka to Shibuya and Setagaya, further characterizing Oyama-kaido as a military road.[2] In 1909, a parade ground and a military prison were installed at Yoyogi, making areas along Oyama-kaido (Aoyama, Yoyogi, and Komazawa) the center of military training in Tokyo's garrison.

## 2-2

## From the Taisho Era to the Prewar and Wartime Years: Meiji Jingu, Army Parade Ground, and Route 246

In 1912, three years after construction of the parade ground, Emperor Meiji passed away, followed by Empress Dowager Shoken in 1914. Accordingly, the construction of Meiji Jingu was planned to enshrine Emperor Meiji and Empress Dowager Shoken. Specifically, a shrine with an inner garden (naien) was built in Minamitoshima District north of Yoyogi Parade Grounds, and an outer garden (gaien) with a memorial picture gallery and athletic facilities were built at Aoyama Parade Grounds [fig.2-2].

The shrine's inner garden, which houses a manmade forest, has received particular treatment as a designated scenic area to protect its landscape.

Yoyogi Parade Grounds began to be used as a venue for military parades near-

[fig.2-2] Japanese reserve soldiers visiting Meiji Jingu (1927)

ly annually under the command of His Majesty Emperor Showa from 1917 through the end of World War II, solidifying its character as a military focal point in the imperial capital [fig.2-3, 2-4]. For civilians, such changes meant an increase of spectators rushing to Yoyogi to see the latest weapons made open to the public in the

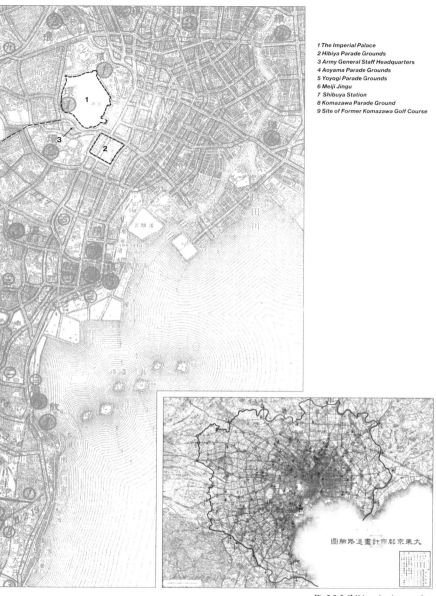

1 The Imperial Palace
2 Hibiya Parade Grounds
3 Army General Staff Headquarters
4 Aoyama Parade Grounds
5 Yoyogi Parade Grounds
6 Meiji Jingu
7 Shibuya Station
8 Komazawa Parade Ground
9 Site of Former Komazawa Golf Course

大東京都市計畫道路綱圖

[fig.2-3, 2-4] Urban planning map of
pre-war Tokyo and military facilities

aforementioned military parades, restaurants and bars flourishing in the area under the patronage of military personnel, and the Shibuya area profiting economically from the military base.[3]

Around 1930, as the Tokyo–Yokohama region recovered from the Great Kanto earthquake of 1923, Hidejiro Nagata (who began serving as Tokyo's mayor the year before the quake) put forward a bid to host the Olympics in the year 2600 of the Japanese imperial calendar (that is, 1940).[4] In July 1936, the International Olympic Committee (IOC) assembling in Berlin decided to hold the 1940 Olympic Games in Tokyo [fig.2-5, 2-6]. Yoyogi, Shinagawa,

[fig.2-5] *Draft of the Olympic gymnasium proposal (February 21, 1935)*

Komazawa, Kamitakaido, and the outer garden of Meiji Jingu were among the nine potential main stadium sites listed during the first Tokyo Olympic Organizing Committee meeting on December 24, 1936. In February 1937, the IOC proposed an expansion of the Meiji Jingu outer garden to house the

[fig.2-6] *Berlin Olympics (photograph by Yoshikazu Uchida)*

swimming pool besides the main stadium, but discussions became overheated and complicated.[5] Serving as an expert in Olympic facility planning at the time, Tokyo Imperial University assistant professor Hideto Kishida had in mind the Yoyogi Parade Grounds (approximately 300,000 tsubo or 991,734m²) as the top candidate besides the outer garden. However, "in a time when militarism reigned supreme, the idea of squandering the imperial army's parade ground for mere sports was all but obliterated."[6] The Bureau of Shrines of the Home Ministry, which managed the district, would not consent, and on April 23, 1938, during its 25th meeting, the Tokyo Olympic Organizing Committee scrapped the plan to reconstruct the outer garden, deciding to construct the main stadium and swimming pool in Komazawa instead [fig.2-7, 2-8].

[fig.2-7] Komazawa Olympic Gymnasium site plan

After the Marco Polo Bridge Incident (July 7, 1937), the Second Sino-Japanese War was drawn into a quagmire, resulting in resource restrictions which made it difficult to obtain steel frames for the main stadium. At the mercy of changing times, Tokyo relinquished its hosting rights for the 1940 Olympic Games on Jul 14, 1938, three months after Komazawa was selected as the main stadium site. Thereafter, the former Komazawa golf course was turned into green

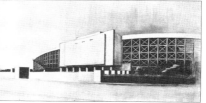

[fig.2-8] Perspective drawing of the façade of the Komazawa Olympic Gymnasium, main facility

space in a 1942 urban planning decision, then acquired by the Tokyo Metropolitan Defense Bureau as air defense green space (September 1943)[7], and planned as the site of the Komazawa Final Defense Field (1943)[8] only to be used as agricultural land to produce food.

In 1938, the year the Tokyo Olympic Games was relinquished, a civil engineer at the Tokyo Metropolitan Government's Capi-

tal City Development Committee named Masao Yamada announced the plan for the Tokyo
Expressway Network. The plan three-dimensionally connected the city center with the airport, railways, canals, and the like, with four
ring roads and eight radial roads (with a total
length of 839km and a width of 16–20m) with an average speed limit of 100km/h. The Tokyo Metropolitan Government had already formulat-
ed a plan for the Greater Tokyo Road Network
(1927), which included Ring Road 7 and 8, but
prospects for implementation looked uncer-
tain. Yamada stressed, "The construction of
expressways is of great urgency, since there
is a likelihood of increase in traffic between
the Tokyo Metropolitan Area and surrounding
cities in the near future from a political, military, and industrial standpoint, and there is a
need to induce decentralization of population
and industry to relieve confliction between urban and rural areas from a regional and national planning viewpoint." [9] It can be pointed out
that Yamada was strongly influenced by Nazi
Germany's national land plan, economic policy
(autarky), and highway system (autobahn) and was
convinced that the astounding development
of the automobile industry would overwhelm
the economic value of railway transport.[10] Yamada had in mind the idea of an expressway
network between Tokyo's vital facilities in the
prewar years, and it was this idea that became
the foundation of the 1957 Metropolitan Expressway Plan.

## 2-3
## Postwar Occupation Policy:
## the Construction
## of Washington Heights

Defeat in World War II extensively affected Tokyo's urban planning. On September 8, 1945,
the 1st Cavalry Division of the US Army set up
camp in Yoyogi[11] on the former army parade
grounds, which was later seized in December
of that year. Afterwards, the US Occupation
ordered the Japanese government to build a
housing district called Washington Heights,
composed of hundreds of residences, ele-
mentary schools, churches, and more for the
US military and their dependents *[fig.2-9, 2-10]*.[12]
As bachelor housing and barracks construction plans for Washington Heights came to
light, the local Shibuya-ku government raised
concerns over unethical behavior and surge in
car traffic. The issue was raised at the House
of Representatives' Foreign Relations Committee, which heard testimonies from the PTA
chairperson of Shibuya-ku's Sanya Elementa-
ry School, a representative from the Shibuya-
ku Yoyogisanya Women's Association, and
Shibuya-ku's Diet members.[13] These protests
were addressed at the third US–Japan Liaison
Conference on November 22, 1955. The US
government expressed a desire to work har-
moniously with the local community and accordingly called for cooperation. As a result,

[fig.2-9] Washington Heights (aerial photograph)

[fig.2-10] Washington Heights Type B-1a, B-2a row houses

66

a local liaison council consisting of both local and US military representatives was set up to meet monthly to address issues.[14] Shibuya-ku persisted in negotiations with the US military, and in late 1958 succeeded in reclaiming the military prison site at the southern end of Washington Heights. Construction of the Shibuya-ku Government Office followed.

On the other hand, the heavy air raids over Tokyo had turned much of the city center to ashes. Hideaki Ishikawa of the Tokyo Metropolitan Government Bureau of Urban Planning, Kenzaburo Kondo of the War Reconstruction Institute, and Yamada and others from the Home Ministry took the lead in drafting a war reconstruction plan. An urban planning decision determined Tokyo's arterial roads, and while discussions were held on the necessity of expressways in Tokyo, such plans remained suspended due to insufficient financial resources. Yamada went on to become director of planning in the Tokyo Metropolitan Government Bureau of Construction in 1955 and emphasized the need for expressways in his report "Roads in Tokyo's Urban Planning, Present and Future"(1956),[15] but prospects for implementation remained bleak.

## 2-4

## The Olympic Bid and
## the Movement to Reclaim
## Washington Heights

In 1952, with war reconstruction ongoing and the US Armed Forces continuing to occupy Yoyogi, the Tokyo Metropolitan Government once again began bidding for the Olympics; the decision to hold the 18th Olympic Games (to begin in 1964) in Tokyo was determined at the 55th IOC Session held in Munich in May 1959 *[fig.2-11]*. As a result, work on Tokyo's urban road network and negotiations for the return of Washington Heights began to take momentum. First, regarding the development of an urban road network, the Tokyo Olympics Prepara-

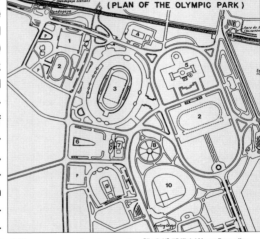

[fig.2-11] *"Official Memo Regarding the 1960 Summer Olympics Bid: Plan of the Olympic Park", Tokyo*

*1 Gymnasium*
*2 Practice Grounds*
*3 Stadium*
*4 Pool*
*5 Art Gallery*
*6 Olympic Park*
*7 National Youth Center*
*8 Sumo Ring*
*9 Pool*

tion Committee decided at the second general meeting held on April 11, 1958, to construct an Olympic Village at Camp Drake in Asaka (formerly an army clothing depot, hereafter Drake). After the bid went through, the committee decided at the third meeting on November 30, 1959, to build on Drake's southern grounds. The "Tokyo Olympic Games Facilities Outline" drafted immediately afterward (December 2, 1959) includes "development of roads interconnecting the Olympic Park, Komazawa Gymnasium, and the Olympic Village as well as roads connecting these places to the city center and Haneda Airport to ensure interconnectivity."[16] In response to the decision to host the Olympics, Yamada declared the necessity for a full review of Tokyo's roads and urban planning in March 1960 and stated the following points: 1, significantly increasing the proportion of road area to total land area; 2, speeding up and adding multilevel crossings to arterial roads by erecting overpasses and underground passages; 3, reorganizing the planned road network economically and efficiently; 4, building off-street parking in urban centers and suburbs, and 5, restricting the building height or building coverage ratio, to prevent rapid increase of traffic demand, in central Tokyo.[17] In addition to the construction of an expressway from Haneda Airport to the city center, the location of the Olympic Village was of particular importance in the construction of the Olympic Road. Because the Olympic Village was planned to be built in Drake, construction of Ring Road 7 connecting Asaka and Komazawa and Radial Route 4 connecting Komazawa and Sendagaya (Oyama-kaido and Route 246) was especially emphasized [fig.2-12].[18]

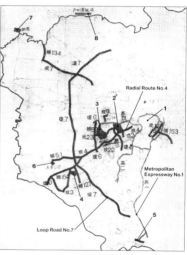

[fig.2-12] Plan for Tokyo 1960 and Olympic facilities

1 The Imperial Palace
2 National Stadium
3 Yoyogi National Gymnasiums
4 Komazawa Stadium
5 Haneda Airport
6 Equestrian Stadium
7 Asaka
8 Toda Rowing Course

It could be said in other words that the Olympic Village was purposely located in Drake to complete Ring Road 7, of which construction was dragging. Regarding the arterial road development to connect Asaka to central Tokyo, the University of Tokyo professor of architecture Eika Takayama points out that recollections of Hitler constructing an expressway on which athletes were driven in military vehicles during the Berlin Olympics may have been at the back of Yamada's mind.[19] Though the development of arterial roads was aimed to make the international festival successful, it also aligned with the national plan to double Japan's national income, advocated by Prime Minister Hayato Ikeda. It was pointed out at the time that the fragility of the city center's infrastructure bottlenecked[20] economic activity and created losses, and arterial road development was expected to serve as the foundation for economic growth.

Meanwhile, regarding the return of Washington Heights, the candidature file (1958) submitted to the IOC by the Japanese Olympic Committee (JOC) specified plans to construct a swimming pool on a site adjacent to Meiji Jingu Stadium (near the current Kasumigaoka apartments).[21] The third Facilities Outline Subcommittee meeting (December 9, 1959) proposed using land at the southern edge of Washington Heights for the gymnasium, and the Ministry of Education requested the return to respective departments. The organizing committee decided during its fourth meeting to build the world's largest swimming pool, with a 40,000-person capacity, in Washington Heights.[22] It would have been most efficient to build both the Olympic Village and the swimming pool in Washington Heights (Yoyogi) if one only considered the movement of athletes between facilities, but the US government had yet to promise its return, and building the village in Drake provided an attractive basis for the construction of Ring Road 7.

However, on May 9, 1961, the US–Japan Joint Committee's special committee on facilities replied that US forces would allow temporary use of but not a fully permanent return of Drake, and it would not allow a partial return of Washington Heights but would allow its full return if the government of Japan fully reimbursed the United States Government for the relocation of their personnel. The US forces' abrupt change in attitude may have been the result of hopes to quell anti-American sentiments resulting from the conflict over the Japan-US Security Treaty which occurred the previous year by returning Yoyogi, a prime locale in central Tokyo, and showing a cooperative stance for the 18th Olympic Games. It would also have been appealing to have the government of Japan pay in full for rebuilding the array of wooden, aging, single-story facilities of Washington Heights.

And so the search for a site on which to build the Olympic Village and swimming pool strayed off. On August 10, 1961, Prime Minister Hayato Ikeda ordered the search for potential locations besides Washington Heights.[23] Consequently, the facility plans developed until that point faced major difficulties and prompted disputes.

Three reasons can be given for this, the first of which is that the Japanese and US governments failed to exchange documentation regarding the return of Washington Heights when Japan bid to host the Olympics. This can be attributed to the lack of equality in diplomacy between the victorious and defeated countries of war. The second being that both the Tokyo Metropolitan Government and Saitama Prefecture were persistent on building the Olympic Village in Asaka because moving the Olympic Village from Asaka to Yoyogi would eliminate the basis for developing Ring Road 7. Third, the government of Japan was reluctant in paying the US government the 8 billion yen required to relocate the American military housing to a hydroponic farm in Chofu.[24] Chichibunomiya Rugby Stadium, Komazawa Athletic Park, Akasaka Rikyu Baseball Stadium, Shinjuku Gyoen, the pool in the Meiji Jingu outer garden, Meiji Park Kasumigaoka, the Shinjuku subcenter, Daikanyama Police Academy, and more[25] were at separate times considered. Unable to find a suitable site in the city center— on October 24, 1961, the government of Japan agreed to the full return of Washington Heights and the establishment of a new swimming pool as well as use of existing facilities for the Olympic Village.[26] The Tokyo Metropolitan Government accepted the Olympic Village relocation on the condition that, first, the metropolitan area's Olympics-related road construction would be completed as planned, and second, Washington Heights would be converted into a forest park. Later, on November 30, 1962, the US military returned a portion of Washington Heights.[27]

In tandem with these intergovernmental talks, the Shibuya-ku Olympic Village Invitational Council (represented by the mayor of Shibuya-ku) and the Olympic Village Invitational Ward Association (a private entity) were established and collected signatures on the street for petitions as part of a grassroots campaign for the return of Washington Heights. Further, the Shibuya-ku Government Office came to include not only the ward office but also Shibuya Public Hall as part of its facilities. That hall was used as the venue for the 18th annual weightlifting competition.

## 2-5
Yoyogi after the Postwar Occupation:
Integration of
the National Gymnasium,
NHK, Kishi Memorial Gymnasium,
and the National Olympics
Memorial Youth Center

One year after the Cabinet's decision to later convert the site of the Olympic Village at the former  Washington Heights to a forest park, NHK requested a partial transfer of Washington Heights. NHK had originally planned to build a TV station in Ryudo-cho, but they deemed the space too small to house a TV and radio broadcast center considering future developments. NHK urged the national government and the capital to sell a portion of Washington Heights amounting to 30,000 tsubo or 99,173m² in August 1962, justifying their claim with a bulk consignment they had contracted with the Tokyo Olympic Organizing Committee.

The Tokyo Metropolitan Government firmly opposed the move, stating that a Cabinet decision had already been made to convert the Olympic Village site into a forest park, and granting NHK's request would create opportunities for other entities to demand land there as well.[28] Subsequently, the national government and Tokyo signed an agreement that took into account the international importance of the broadcasting business with regard to the Olympics, agreeing on the following: 1, the national government would provide NHK with land within 25,000 tsubo or 82,645m² of the preplanned forest park; 2, all land excluding the aforementioned would be designated as a forest park; and 3, the national government would loan the Tokyo Metropolitan Government, free of charge, state-owned land roughly equivalent in area to the portion of Washington Heights provided to the NHK broadcast center. As a result, the Tokyo Metropolitan Government was freely loaned roughly 9,000 tsubo or 29,752m² of state-owned land in Shinryudo-cho in Aoyama Park as well as the former Maeda residence in Komaba-cho, Meguro-ku (currently Komaba Park, roughly 9,800 tsubo or 32,397m²).[29]

In turn, while the Kishi Memorial Gymnasium in Ochanomizu had become well-renowned as a hub for amateur sports, in May 1963, a decision was made to relocate it to Washington Heights. Approximately 5400m² of state-owned land situated between the Yoyogi National Gymnasium and the Yamanote line side was disposed at a price of 180,000 Yen per tsubo or 3.3m², the same as that of the NHK broadcast center.

In terms of size, 1 basement level and 4 levels aboveground with a floor area of 10,000m² were planned, with rooms for IOC members of respective countries, organizing committee offices, respective sports federation offices, and domestic and international press rooms. Consequently, the Olympic Village, the Yoyogi National Gymnasium as the venue for swimming and basketball, the Shibuya Public Hall as the weightlifting venue, and the NHK broadcast center entrance were all concentrated on the Washington Heights site.

Massive traffic was to be expected from spectator activity and the convergence of Olympic related vehicles, and thus in February 1964, plans were drafted and implemented to prepare a large plaza at the Shibuya Exit to the Olympic Village and to improve Tokyo Metropolitan Road Route 155, an auxiliary road in Tokyo's urban planning road development.[30]

Because the Shibuya-ku Government Office, the Shibuya Public Hall, and NHK each had various views and interests differing from that of the gymnasium, there was no room for discussion or way to reach a mutual agreement. Tange regrets, "The Shibuya Exit Plaza is not only completely visually unstructured, functional problems like the separation of pedestrian and vehicle traffic have been left unresolved."[31]

Further, fifteen 4-story, reinforced concrete barracks remained on the northern edge of Washington Heights. At the end of April 1964, the Ministry of Education envisioned establishing a National Olympic Memorial Youth Center using these buildings, and consulted the Ministry of Finance.[32] It was planned to be

a site of international exchange — group training and guidance for young athletes through
physical education and sports, instructor
training in physical education and sports,
and short-term accommodation for young
foreign nationals during international competitions and other international exchanges.
Other applications included providing a facility for guidance necessary to develop group
action in social education events and educa-
tional excursions. Although proposals for use
of the land by the Japan Housing Corporation
as well as for a National Tax Agency training
office were rumored immediately after the
Olympics,[33] the youth center was established
in 1965 and began accepting trainees the following year.

1 "Etchujima-gawa kasen seibi kihon hoshin [Basic Policy on Etchujima-gawa River Improvement]," Tokyo Metropolitan Government Bureau of Construction, 2005, 2.

2 Ritsuto Yoshida, "Dai 9-sho: Shibuya shuhen no gunji-teki kukan no keisei [Chapter 9: Formation of Military Spaces around Shibuya]," Rekishi no naka no Shibuya 2: Shibuya kara Edo, Tokyo he [Shibuya in History 2: From Shibuya to Edo and Tokyo], ed. Kazuo Ueyama (Tokyo: Yuzankaku, 2011), 252.

3 Ritsuto Yoshida, "Dai 2-sho: Yoyogi renpeijo no shakai-shi [Chapter 2: The Social History of Yoyogi Parade Grounds]," Shibuya gaku sosho dai 5-kan: Shibuya: Nigiwai kukan wo kagaku suru [Shibuya Studies, Book 5: Shibuya: Scientifically Studying a Busy Space], ed. Kazuo Ueyama (Tokyo: Yuzankaku, 2017), 78.

4 Kazuo Hashimoto, Maboroshi no Tokyo Orinpikku [The Imaginary Tokyo Olympics], (Tokyo: NHK Publishing, 1994).

5 Ibid., 150-151.

6 Hideto Kishida, "Orinpikku Tokyo taikai to sono shisetsu [Tokyo Olympic Games and Its Facilities],"Shin-kenchiku [New Architecture], October 1964, 117.

7 "Komazawa kouen ni kansuru shiryo [Documents Pertaining to Komazawa Park]," Miyako-shi shiryo shusei II, dai 7-kan: Orinpikku to Tokyo [Tokyo History Collection II, Vol. 7: The Olympics and Tokyo, ed. Tokyo Metropolitan Archives, Tokyo Metropolitan Cultural Affairs Bureau, 2018, 361.

8 Toshitaro Minomo, "Setagaya-ku ni okeru koen seibi no suii ni kansuru kenkyu [A Study on Changes to Park Construction in Setagaya Ward]," Zoen zasshi [Landscaping Magazine], 54(5) 1991, 324.

9 Masao Yamada, "Tokyo kosoku doro-mo keikaku-an gaiyo [Tokyo Expressway Network Plan Overview]," Toki no nagare, toshi no nagare [The Flow of Time, the Flow of a Capital] (Tokyo: Kajima Institute Publishing, 1973), 118. (First publication: City Planning Tokyo Regional Committee, 1938.)

10 Masao Yamada, "Dai 1-sho: 1937–1941: Jidosha jidai, daitoshi jidai no torai [Chapter 1: 1937–1941: The Arrival of the Era of Automobiles and the Era of the Metropolis]," Toki no nagare, toshi no nagare [The Flow of Time, the Flow of a Capital] (Tokyo: Kajima Institute Publishing, 1973), 5.

11 "Ichiya ni 'tenmaku-mura' shutsugen: Yoyogi renpeijo setsuei no dai ichi-nichi ['Tent Village' Emerges Overnight: The First Day of Yoyogi Parade Grounds Construction]", Asahi Shimbun, September 10, 1945.

12 "Yoyogi ni beigun jutaku-mura: raihaido, gekijo made kan-

bi [US Military Residential Village in Yoyogi: Chapel, Theater Complete]," Asahi Shimbun, September 10, 1946.

13  House of Representatives Foreign Relations Committee No. 11, February 27, 1954.

14  "Mondai kaiketsu: Shoko, gunzoku kyuhyaku ga nyukyo Washinton Haitsu_Tokyoto [Problem Solving: 900 Officers, Military Personnel Move In to Washington Heights_Tokyo-to], Asahi Shimbun, November 23, 1955.

15  Akira Koshizawa, "12-Sho Tokyo Orinpikku to shuto kosoku doro [Chapter 12: The Tokyo Olympics and the Metropolitan Expressway]," Tokyo toshi keikaku monogatari [A Tale of Tokyo City Planning], (Tokyo: Nihon Keizai Hyoronsha, 1991), 225.

16  Ministry of Education, Culture, Sports, Science and Technology, "Dai 4-sho: Kyoryoku no ikisatsu to sono naiyo [Chapter 4: Background and Details of Cooperation]," Orinpikku Tokyo Taikai to seifu kikan to no kyoryoku [Tokyo Olympic Games and Cooperation between Government Agencies], 1965, 61.

17  Masao Yamada, "Tokyo Orinpikku to kotsu mondai [The Tokyo Olympics and Traffic Issues]," Shin-toshi [The New City], March 1960, 9.

18  "Especially regarding Radial Route 4, there are numerous difficulties such as the arrangement of Aoyama-dori's dense shopping strip, Shibuya–Sangenjaya's relationship with the Tamagawa train; the solution would be difficult to achieve without aggressive adoption of methods such as large-scale national and capital city expenditures, obviously, as well as multilevel replotting, mid- to high-tier financing for finance corporations, and the Housing Corporation's construction of housing facilities in urban areas." Hideo Kimura, "Orinpikku Tokyo taikai wo mukaeru tame ni [To Welcome the Tokyo Olympic Games]," Shin-toshi [The New City], March 1960, 4.

19  Eika Takayama, Toshi no ryoiki: Takayama eika no shigoto [Urban Areas: Takayama Eika's Work], Kenchikuka Kaikan Series (Tokyo: Kenchikuka Kaikan, 1997), 85-86.

20  "Economic growth requires basic infrastructure, but there is a considerable bottleneck in transportation and telecommunications, and this blocking the economy's development became a theme. So the elimination of bottlenecks in roads, rail, and telecommunications has become a major issue in national land policy." Atsushi Shimokobe, "Dai 3-kai: Sengo 50-nen no kokudo kaihatsu [3: Land Development 50 Years after the War]," Kokudo gyosei keikaku ko [National Land Management Plan Considerations] (Tokyo: Japan Institute of Country-ology and Engineering, 2002), 4.

21 "Dai 18-kai Orinpikku kyogi taikai rikkoho fairu fuzu: PLAN FOR THE OLYMPIC PARK [18th Olympic Games Candidate File Figure: PLAN FOR THE OLYMPIC PARK]," Miyako-shi shiryo shusei II, dai 7-kan: Orinpikku to Tokyo [Tokyo History Collection II, Vol. 7: The Olympics and Tokyo], ed. Tokyo Metropolitan Archives, Tokyo Metropolitan Cultural Affairs Bureau, 2018, frontispiece.

22 "Washinton Haitsu Yoyogi ni kimaru: sekai saidai gorin-yo puru [Decided, Washington Heights Yoyogi: World's Largest Olympic Pool]" Yomiuri Shimbun, January 30, 1960.

23 "Gorin taiikukan chu ni uku: Washinton Haitsu ha dannen, shusho shiji de hoka wo busshoku [Olympic Gymnasium in the Air: Washington Heights Abandoned, Seeking Other Options under Prime Minister's Directive]," Asahi Shimbun, morning edition, August 11, 1961.

24 Masaji Tabata quotation. "20 Seiki no kiseki: gorin urabanashi (zoku) 46: Yoyogi senshu mura[Tracks of the 20th Century: Behind the Scenes of the Olympics (Continued) 46: Yoyogi Olympic Village]," Asahi Shimbun, September 19, 1984.

25 Tokyo Olympic Organizing Committee, Orinpikku Tokyo taikai, shiryoshu 7: shisetsu-bu [Tokyo Olympic Games, Collection 7: Facilities Department], 1965, 11.

26 "Zenmen henkan moshiire: Washinton Haitsu [Full Refund Request: Washington Heights]," Asahi Shimbun, morning edition, October 25, 1961.

27 "Asu, ichibu henkan, Washinton Haitsu [Partial Return of Washington Heights Tomorrow]," Asahi Shimbun, morning edition, November 29, 1962.

28 "Togikai: seifu yosei ni hantai, NHK terebi senta Yoyogi-hara he no kensetsu [Tokyo Metropolitan Assembly: Opposition to Government Request, Construction of NHK Broadcasting Center in Yoyogihara]" Asahi Shimbun, January 15, 1963.

29 Sadaharu Aikawa, Rokuro Fuse, Yoyogi koen [Yoyogi Park], Tokyo-to koen kyokai kanshu, Tokyo Koen 27 (Tokyo: Gogakusha, 1981), 30.

30 Ministry of Education, Culture, Sports, Science and Technology Vol. 6, "Yoyogi senshu-mura Shibuya-guchi zenmen hiroba no seibi ni tsuite [Regarding Preparation of the Entire Yoyogi Olympic Village Shibuya Exit Plaza]," decided February 12, 1964, recipient: director of the Ministry of Construction Kanto Construction Bureau, sender: director of the Ministry of Education, Culture, Sports, Science and Technology Physical Education Bureau, National Archives.

31 Kenzo Tange, "Kokuritsu okunai sogo kyogi-jo no keiken [Na-

tional Indoor Stadium Experiences]," Kenchiku bunka [Architectural Culture], January 1965, *75*.

32 Ministry of Education, Culture, Sports, Science and Technology Vol. 168, "Orinpikku senshu-mura no taikai shuryogo no shiyo ni tsuite [Regarding the Use of the Olympic Village after the Olympics]," decided May 1, 1964, recipient: director of the Ministry of Finance Bureau of Trustees, sender: director of the Ministry of Education, Culture, Sports, Science and Technology Physical Education Bureau, National Archives of Japan.

33 "Yakkaina atoshimatsu: Orinpikku [Troublesome Cleanup: the Olympics]" Nikkei, evening edition, October 25, 1964.

# 3

# Yoyogi National Gymnasium Understood through Architectural Design

The Yoyogi National Gymnasium (named National Indoor Stadium in its planning stages) has a site area of approximately 91,022m²; a structure consisting of reinforced concrete, steel-reinforced concrete, and a high-tension cable suspended roof; 2 basement levels and 2 levels above ground; a total floor area approximating 27,507m² in the 1st gymnasium, 4,862m² in adjoining rooms, and 5,675m² in the 2nd gymnasium; and a capacity of 11,593 people in the 1st gymnasium and 3,545 in the 2nd (not including standing room). The cost of the construction is approximately 3,060 million Yen, and the work was undertaken by Shimizu Corporation (1st gymnasium) and Obayashi Corporation (2nd gymnasium) [Fig.3-1–4].

The stadium's design was a collaboration between Kenzo Tange (architectural design), Yoshikatsu Tsuboi (structural engineering), and Uichi Inouye (facilities engineering), and preliminary and working designs were completed in approximately 12 months. The Ministry of Construction estimated the plan would require a construction period of at least 22 months, but temporary construction began on site in February 1963 with strict orders to deliver by the end of August 1964. As a result, a short period of only 19 months were given to complete the challenging structure.

[fig.3-1] Exterior of Yoyogi National Gymnasium, 1st gymnasium, at the time of completion

[fig.3-2] Interior of Yoyogi National Gymnasium, 1st gymnasium, at the time of completion

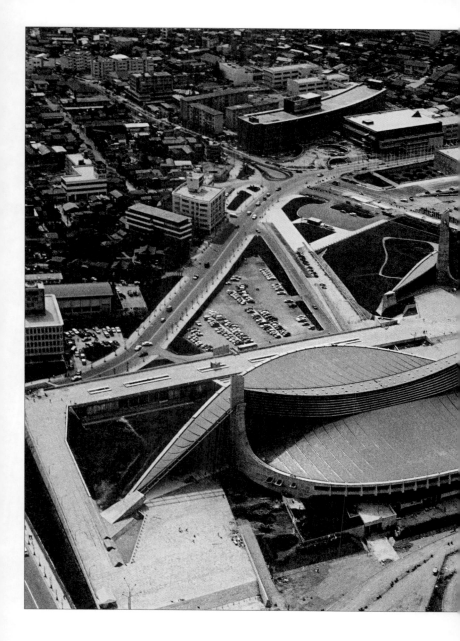

84

[fig.3-3] Yoyogi National Gymnasium
at the time of completion
(aerial photograph)

# 3-1
## The Design Process of Yoyogi National Gymnasium

### 1. Selection of the Architect

The Ministry of Education coordinated with the Ministry of Construction and the organizing committee members to discuss the design process for the National Indoor Stadium design on multiple occasions. As a result, it was decided that a committee be established in the Ministry of Education to select and nominate excellent, internationally recognized candidates among the domestic architects, following the design selection process of other national buildings of special importance. And thus, the committee tasked with selecting the architect for the National Indoor Stadium, comprising special chairperson Hideto Kishida, executives from the Ministry of Education and Ministry of Construction as well as 13 other experts, were summoned to the Ministry of Education's Sports and Culture Bureau room on November 13 and 20, 1961.

In April 1961, the Ministry of Education had expected that the preliminary designs would be completed by late October of the same year. But being unable to settle on an architect in mid-November, they stood the risk of failing to complete the building before the Tokyo Olympic Games were held, unless they began imme-

[fig.3-4] *Exterior of Yoyogi National Gymnasium, 2nd gymnasium, at the time of completion*

Yoyogi National Gymnasium Understood through Architectural Design

diately. Therefore, due to an urgent situation which lacked sufficient time for a competition, the selection committee chose a discretionary contract in accordance with the budget settlement of the provisions in Article 29 of the Accounting Law under Article 96 of the Accounting Order. Considering past achievements, the committee selected a design group comprising Kenzo Tange, Yoshikatsu Tsuboi, and Uichi Inouye, to draft the preliminary designs.

In January 1962, it was decided that site surveys of the area planned for the National Indoor Stadium be conducted from late January to late February, and the Construction Engineering Research Society Foundation was selected as the contractor for the preliminary designs. This foundation, approved by the Ministry of Education, primarily engaged in research and development related to architectural and civil engineering, and many serving the foundation had previously supported Tsuboi's structural engineering design. A system was set up wherein the foundation served as the parent organization, and Tange, Tsuboi, and Inouye drafted the preliminary designs under the organization. The preliminary design fees amounted to 4.8 million yen compared to construction fees of 2.24531 billion yen. On May 11, 1962, the organizing committee convened, and there the design outline and construction plan outlines were discussed and then printed in the newspapers the following morning.

Immediately thereafter, the process to select the contractor for the working designs began and ultimately favored Urtec (Urbanists and Architects), a design team to which Tange served as an advisor. The Ministry of Education cited three reasons for selecting Urtec. First, the Ministry of Construction was busy building military housing in Chofu and could spare no resources, leaving the Ministry of Education no choice but to outsource the National Indoor Stadium's working design to a private design firm. Second, major design firms did not usually produce working designs based on another firms' preliminary designs. Third, it was stated that the working design of this stadium would require, consistency and faithful adherence to the particularities of the preliminary design and a contractor capable of satisfying the contract conditions organization-wise and ability-wise.

Previous research indicates a tug-of-war situation between the Ministry of Construction—who wanted to design the Yoyogi National Gymnasium—and Kishida—who recommended Tange to produce the designs. No evidence of confliction could be confirmed between Kishida and the Ministry of Construction in public documents, but it could be interpreted that the Ministry of Education—torn between the Ministry of Construction's own desire to design the facility and Kishida's endorsement of Tange—proposed a mediation by contriving three reasons for the selection of the designer. Some desired a competition, but time was limited and it was deemed impractical.

Tange having previously conducted his designs at the Tange Laboratory of the Department of Architecture at the University of Tokyo, moved his base of design operations to Urtec after having been assigned as the preliminary designer of the National Indoor Stadium, to clear any doubts of dual employment. Because Tange was a faculty member of a national university which is a public servant, Koji Kamiya (who directed the Tange Laboratory) became president of Urtec as well as the planning notification application representative.

At the time, according to the schedule prepared by the Ministry of Education, the working designs were to be completed by late September 1962, the costs to be estimated in October or November, the bidding to take place at year's end, with construction to begin in January 1963, and the building to be completed in late August 1964. At this stage, completion by October 1963 was unrealistic, indicating that the schedule had become so tight, that the structure could only be completed immediately before the Olympics.

## 2. Preliminary Design

Having been named as the designers, Tange, Tsuboi, and Inouye took to drafting the preliminary design. The design process was considered through various study models constructed by the Tange Laboratory, responsible for the architectural design [fig.3-5-8]. The "National Indoor Stadium Preliminary Design Guide" that they submitted to the Ministry of Education on March 20, 1962, included seven parts (architectural outline, area table, finish table, architectural design guide, structural design guide, facilities design guide, and construction fees estimate). Here an overview of the architectural, structural, and facilities design guides and the construction fees estimate is presented.

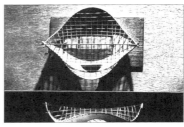

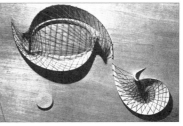

The first part, the architectural design guide, was organized into three sections: A. General, B. Layout Plan, and C. Architectural Plan. Section A. General, describes the goal of constructing a high standard ten thousand–person capacity Olympic stadium on an international level, where the large crowd of spectators and athletes can become one in taking part in the athletic competition and which provides a dynamic space that enhances a feeling of international unity among the unanimous excitement.

[fig.3-5-8] Study model of Yoyogi National Gymnasium during the preliminary design stage

Section B. Layout Plan states that the center of the 1st gymnasium be placed simultaneously on the axis connecting Shibuya Station and Meiji Jingu shrine and on the approximate north-south axis (the axis on which the Meiji Jingu

Shrine is arranged) *[fig.3-9]*. The small gymnasium was set westerly on the site to balance with the 1st gymnasium. Additionally, a promenade connecting the Harajuku Exit and Shibuya Exit was constructed between the parking lot and the gymnasium. The aim of this layout was to lead visitors from Harajuku and Shibuya station as well as visitors coming by car to a single gate.

[fig.3-9] Site plan at the time of completion

1 Main Gymnasium
2 Sub Gymnasium
3 NHK
4 Shibuya General Government Building
5 Kishi Memorial Gymnasium

Section C. Architectural Plan states that the 1st gymnasium's primary entrance face both the Harajuku and Shibuya Exits, from which spectators can reach their seats by following either an upward or downward slope. Because it was a tomoe-shaped plan (tomoe being a comma-like heraldic design), visitors could see the entire arena and the spectator seats from the main entrance and thereby quickly find their seats. Spectator seats were arranged so that the edges of the pool could be seen from each seat. In the 1st gymnasium arena, a 22m × 50m swimming pool and a 22m × 50m diving pool were installed. Movable floor panels and movable pipes could be placed over the pool enabling the facility to be used as a 28m × 60m ice skating rink. The 2nd gymnasium housed a basketball court and spectator seats which could be partially removed to reveal an additional court that could be used during practice. This flexibility was also to consider usage of the gymnasium for other purposes.

The second part, the structural design guide by Tsuboi and Kawaguchi Mamoru (who worked with Tsuboi on structural designs), was organized into three sections: types of suspended roofs, a review of the applicability of various types of structures, and soil and foundation properties and appropriate countermeasures. First, the suspended roofs are divided into seven types (1, a unidirectional type like Dulles International Airport by Saarinen; 2, a bidirectional type like Nowicki's J. S. Dorton Arena; 3, a radial type like E.D. Stone's American pavilion at the Brussels World's Fair; 4, a catenary arch type like in Ingalls Rink by Saarinen; 5, a yet unrealized ridged net type structure; 6, a suspended roof type like G. Kirchner's Frankfurt aircraft hangar; and 7, other roof types illustrated by Seidler's Olympic Stadium in Melbourne) [fig.3-9−20].

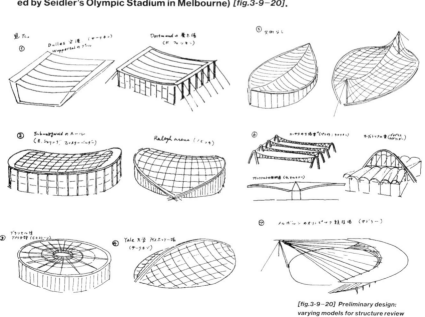

[fig.3-9−20] Preliminary design: varying models for structure review

Of the seven types, Tsuboi and Kawaguchi set their sights on 5, the yet unrealized ridged net type structure, as a major element in their preliminary design, and set about specifically reviewing leaf-shaped suspended roofs [fig. 3-21] and tower-type roofs [fig.3-22]. For the former's boundary arch, plane and spatial curves were examined. As illustrated in Fig.3-21, the main cable (ridged net) would extend between A1 and A2 (120m span), and after the installation of secondary parabolic concrete arches passing through A1, A3, and A2, sub-cables would be suspended between these arches and the main cables to form a roof. The aim of the design was to balance the ridged net structure's tensile force with the thrust (lateral load) from the parabolic concrete arches in a ring configuration. Although Tsuboi and Kawaguchi evaluated the design to be structurally rational, it did not match Tange's vision.

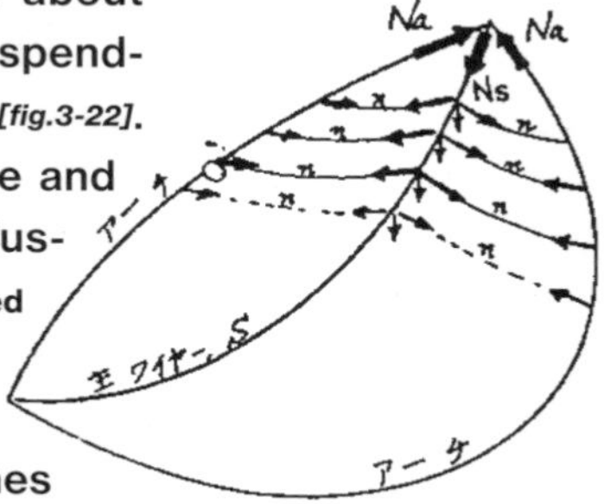

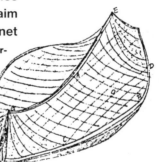

[fig.3-21] Leaf-shaped suspended roof

[fig.3-22] Pole-type roof

The latter, the pole-type roof [fig.3-22], required the installation of two poles or towers; between these, the main cable (ridged net) would be suspended like in any suspension bridge, and the numerous sub-cables extending from both sides of the main cable toward the spectator seats (forming a secondary net) would form the roof. Unlike shell structures, a suspended roof's boundaries, loads, and tensile strength mechanically determine a suspended roof's curvature, making arbitrary curves impossible to construct. Thus, a mechanically viable shape must initially be given. Decisions regarding the curvature was of particular importance in ridged net structures, since though the main cable (ridged net) itself fulfills a boundary type of role, a change in the tension of sub-cables (the secondary net) changes the form of the main cable (ridged net), thereby affecting the tension of other sub-cables. Tsuboi deemed the pole-type suspended roof a suitable model for the design, stating that it was possible to create something close to the designer's vision using mechanically rational curved surfaces and at the same time keeping the internal forces with an allowable range. He added that the model was worth pursing in design, despite the new obstacles in analysis and engineering that may arise due to the relatively short history of suspended roofs as well as the issue of the construction deadline.

The third part, the facilities design guide, organizes its topics into water supply and drainage and sanitary equipment, pool filtration and humidification systems, ice skating rink facilities, HVAC, the electrical system, the lighting system, and the motor power system.

Regarding the pool filtration and humidification system, water was to circulate through the swimming, diving, and practice pools in 3.5, 13.5, and 3.5 hours, respectively. Meanwhile, air conditioning would be restricted to offices, executive offices, and VIP rooms. Spectator seats would have mechanical ventilation and warm air heating only, and the athletes' waiting areas would be directly heated with radiators. In fact, saddle-shaped roof structures, like the one planned here, reduce the air conditioning load compared to dome-shaped gymnasiums, and have an acoustically advantageous shape in reducing echoes. On the other hand, budgetary constraints likely left the spectator seating areas uncooled.

The fourth part, the construction fees estimate, is divided into architectural construction fees, electrical system installation fees, competition-related equipment fees, construction field office installation fees, and site preparation and survey fees. Total construction fees were estimated at 2.2 billion Yen in the document "National Indoor Stadium Preliminary Design Guide" (March 20, 1962). Notes on another document enclosed with the former ("National Indoor Stadium Preliminary Design Progress and Requests," May 8, 1962) states, "Tabata: 15,000–12,000, Tange: reduced due to budget, Fukuya: 90cm by 40cm per seat, Tokyo: residential area, building greater than 20m in height requires prior discussion." This suggests that the pool facility's capacity was decreased in consideration of a reduced budget and seat size.

## 3. Working Design

On October 5, 1962, the Tsuboi Yoshikatsu Structural Design Office compiled the "National Indoor Stadium Structural Calculations,

1." Because it was written immediately after the working design was completed, the contents of the document likely follow those of the working design submitted to the Ministry of Construction. Here, for the 1st gymnasium, the main cables are suspended between two primary reinforced concrete (RC) towers installed 120m apart like in a suspension bridge *[fig.3-23]*. A hanging net structure is suspended from these main cables to the RC base of the gymnasium. A restraining net structure is then cast perpendicularly to the cable net structure to construct a ridged curved surface, over which steel sheets are installed to form a roof. Additionally, the number of main cables had been increased from the preliminary design to two. The main cables are combined with a steel truss to form a monitor roof and the steel roofing sheets are stiffened with ribs (with long I-beams) to provide sufficient flexural rigidity to resist variable loads from wind and snow. Since the effect of the restraining net structure is small where the curvature is especially small near the center of the gymnasium roof, the depth of the stiffening ribs on the steel roofing sheets is continuously increased at this location.

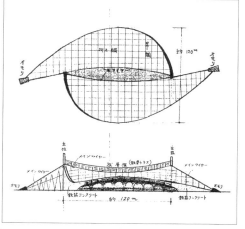

[fig.3-23] 1st gymnasium roof working floor plan, elevation

Actual construction methods, however,

had not yet been reviewed in this proposal. To begin with, a tightly stretched roof (a curved surface where the intersecting hanging and restraining net structures are both under tension but have opposite principal curvatures, resulting in a negative Gaussian curvature) formed from the boundary condition consisting of the main cables and the three-dimensionally undulating RC base (the gymnasium's structural perimeter) may theoretically exist. But attempting to achieve this with only three types of cables (netting) required the difficult technique of applying excessive tension to an area of the restraining net. But attempting to achieve this with only three types of cables or nets (main cables, hanging net, restraining net) requires the application of excessive tension in a portion of the restraining net, resulting in an extreme difficulty in construction. Regardless of the anxieties surrounding this issue, construction began for a roof constructed from a combination of a hanging net and restraining net forming a cable network, with supporting ribs along the suspended net to resist variable nonuniform wind, snow, and seismic loads, as determined in the final drafting stages of the working design. It was then that Kawaguchi, taking part in the structural engineering under Tsuboi, proposed an inspiring plan called a semi-rigid roof structure, to which Tsuboi agreed.

As for the 2nd gymnasium, its main cable is hung from the top of the main tower to the edge of the gymnasium's spiral shaped RC base, and from this main cable, a steel truss (depth of 600mm) extends radially to the upper part of the base. The suspended steel truss not only functions as a tension member but also provides flexural rigidity to resist variable loads. The steel sheet roofing here is the same as the 1st gymnasium's.

As in the drafting stages of the preliminary design, the 1st gymnasium floor plan in the working design is an open configuration formed of two offset crescents; the 2nd gymnasium is arranged to correspond with this [fig.3-24]. This layout is planned to smoothly accommodate the movements of large crowds, emphasizing approaches from the Harajuku and Shibuya Exits. In a significant departure from the preliminary design, the gymnasiums connect via the office building's passage space stretching east to west, taking advantage of the site's varying elevations.

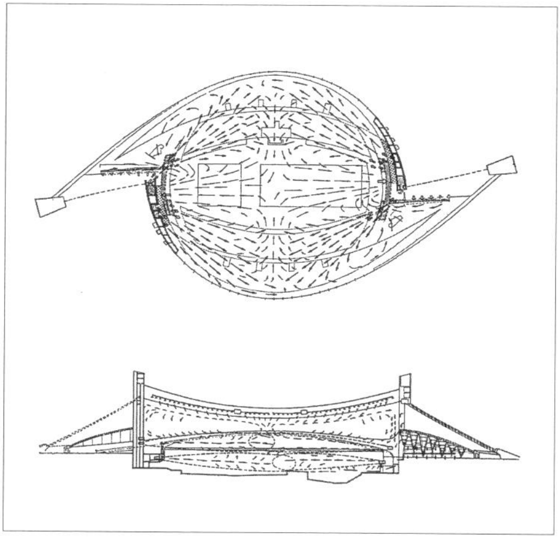

[fig.3-24] *Floor plan showing air circulation, Sectional showing air circulation*

Inouye, who led facilities engineering, offered three exemplary methods to air condition large spaces. The first involved air conditioning via the plenum by erecting large ducts from an air conditioning equipment room in the basement floor. The second involved hanging exposed air conditioning units from the ceiling, but the method was problematic in terms of design. The third called for a large air conditioner installed in the plenum. However, all of these methods presented the possibility of producing noise and vibration and so were abandoned. As a result, 16 large nozzles were installed in the 1st gymnasium's exterior walls to send 500,000m³ of air per hour to 140,000 spectators. The advantage of this method was that it eliminated the need for air conditioning units or ductwork in the ceiling, simplifying maintenance and avoiding difficulties from noise and vibration. Since few precedents existed, Inouye et al. experimented repeatedly with large models to complete the implementation [fig.3-25–27].

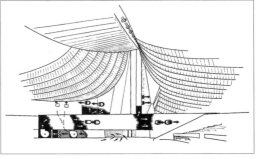

[fig.3-25] Nozzle locations in the 1st gymnasium

 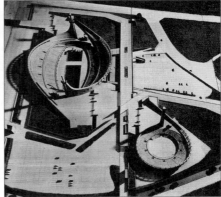

[fig.3-26, 3-27] Photograph of models at the end of the working design phase

# 3-2
# The Construction Process of
# Yoyogi National Gymnasium

## 1. The Five Obstacles to Site Management

Kaichi Negishi, who (as a member of the Ministry of Construction) served as a site manager on the Yoyogi National Gymnasium project, cites five obstacles that would affect the construction progress on the 1st gymnasium.[1]

The first obstacle would present itself due to the utterly unknown difficulties of installing an unprecedented suspended roof *[fig.3-28]*. The second obstacle would involve the three-sided posts that support the cantilever like edges of the RC gymnasium stands until the steel beams, placed at 4.5m intervals to constitute the hanging net structure, were connected between the main cables and cantilevered edge of the RC base, lifting the latter. The aluminum

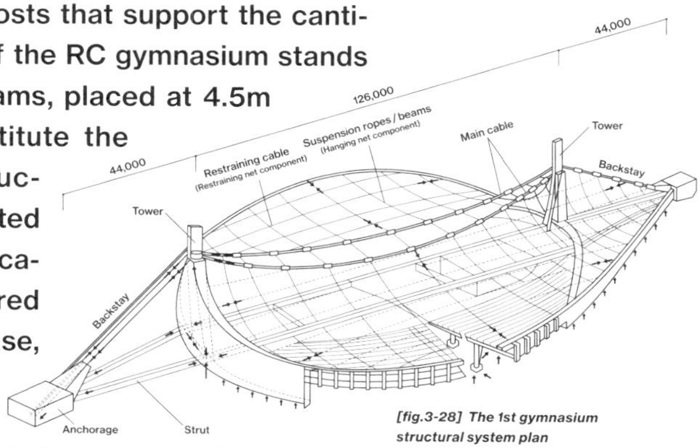

[fig.3-28] The 1st gymnasium structural system plan

door and window fittings around the exterior would be installed only after the three-sided posts are removed. The third obstacle would be the inability to construct the complicated ceiling without first constructing the roof with its equally complicated curved surface.

The fourth obstacle would be the indoor scaffolding exceeding 30m in height required to construct the roof; until the scaffolding is removed, construction on the pool cannot begin. The fifth obstacle was the coincidence of exterior construction with the rainy season, and the difficulty of calculating how long embankment work using Kanto loam (soil local to the Kanto region) would take.

## 2. Marking (February 1962) and Foundation Work (March–July 1962)

The geometry of the 1st gymnasium's layout is determined by combining a circle and a sine curve. Because the column positions in particular depend on the intersection of curved and straight lines, the task of marking required a week using computers.[2] On site, the angle and distance were calculated from 9m grid-based reference points. The distance was measured with a Riverstone steel tape measure (50m long with units of 1mm and values added for temperature correction), pulled with a tensile force of 10kg during the survey. The lengths of crucial components were always measured on site using steel tape measures matched with this particular tape measure.

The gymnasium's foundation was reinforced in three ways: H-piles, pedestal piles, and isolated footing. H-piles were installed to support large loads, such as the two towers and the hinged-base column foundation.

H-piles 22–24.3m in length, are joined in pairs, and have a life cycle of 100 years (i.e., the pile's load capacity will drop to design value after 100 years). Forty-seven H-piles were installed under one tower, with a total of 425 installed for the whole gymnasium.

Pedestal piles are installed primarily in the foundation of the lower section of the gymnasium base as well as the foundation of the lobby columns; measuring 16–29m long, 514 of them were used in the construction of the 1st gymnasium. Isolated footing was employed only where the building protruded from the main structure as well as for the adjacent single-story building, and are separated using expansion joints. Although the soil boring test results revealed no apparent problems, settlement occurred at several locations after the completion of construction. This is considered to have occurred due to substantial compressive force acting within the Kanto loam.[3]


3. Concrete Construction
   (July 1963–March 1964)

As mentioned during discussion of the second obstacle to construction, the cantilever like edges of the RC gymnasium stand was supported by three-sided steel posts, and all else was supported by pipe scaffolding [fig.3-29–32]. Because these three-sided posts were to each bear approximately 49t for long periods of time, it was necessary to calculate

[fig.3-29] *Pouring concrete into the 1st floor spectator seating area forms*

[fig.3-30] *Pouring concrete into the 1st floor spectator seating area forms*

in advance the load-bearing capacity of concrete slabs and embankments that would support the posts, as well as perform rolling com-
paction and careful planning. Settlement was
constantly measured through the use of piano
wires lowered from the upper columns.[4]

For the formwork, since most of the 1st
gymnasium's base was exposed concrete involving complicated
curved surfaces, nu-
merous materials
were prepared
and their finishes and construction fees were reviewed.
Emphasizing in particular the
use of only a sin-
gle type of material, it was decided to employ
veneer (with a base 12mm and composite 3mm thick),
but the veneer base proved too thin, leading
to mishaps on site. Japanese lime, Japanese
beech, and lauan plywood were considered,
but the use of plywood made of ordinary veneer coated with stolon resin was ultimately
decided on.

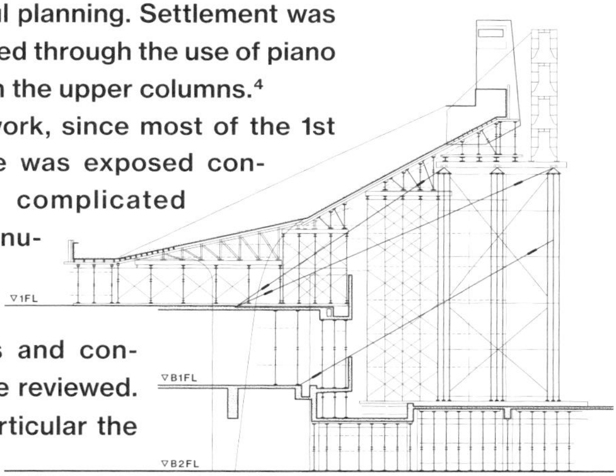

The floor of the RC gymnasium, made of
three-dimensionally arched, curved surfaces,
was impossible to describe in its entirety in
drawings because the layout was point sym-
metric and the shapes nonuniform and varying. Therefore, formwork for one section of
the arch was built in full scale in advance, and
many meetings with the designer were held.

The precision with which the formwork

[fig.3-31] Shores supporting the 1st
gymnasium spectator seating area

*[fig.3-32] Pos supporting the 1st gymnasium stand*

was installed was set at 2/1000 for those to be finished and 1/1000 for exposed columns. The deepest concern regarding formwork safety involved the slope of the gymnasium base; the downward, diagonal force of the pouring concrete may apply horizontal forces to the formwork. No one could estimate the magnitude of this force, and so the scaffolding was reinforced with braces to the fullest extent to ensure safety.[5]

## 4. Preparation of the Components
   for the Suspended Roof

Wire ropes are used for the main cables and restraining net structure in the 1st gymnasium. The wires that compose them are equivalent to Class 1 JIS G 3502-1960 piano wire rods (SWRSIA).[6] Regarding the rope's lay, the 1st gymnasium employed lang lay rope — often used in main ropes in mines and cableways due to its high flexibility and fatigue resistance — because it would only be subject to static loads and not be worn down.

The approximately 280m long main cable comprises 31 A ropes and 6 B ropes, with 127 wires twisted to form the 52ø A rope and 61 wires twisted for the 34.5ø B rope. At 44ø, the ropes in the restraining net structure consists of 91 wires. Since these wire ropes can unwind, they are first pretensioned for two hours at approximately half the guaranteed failure load before their lengths are measured under the application of the design load. With this procedure, the ropes' elastic modulus was increased and its kinks removed. Further, because temperature and direct sunlight can expand or contract the rope's length, the ropes underwent this process in the early morning or cloudy or rainy days when the effect of solar heat is minimal.[7]

Cast iron played a crucial role in the 1st gymnasium's suspended roof. Tasked with its structural engineering, Tsuboi, Kawaguchi, et al. created numerous ingenious components to adapt to the many complex features of the main cables and suspended steel beams. Among them, the development of the saddle and the spherical band are particularly noteworthy. The saddle set at the top of the towers enabled a mechanism for the main cables on top of the tower to move smoothly as the cable moved, sagged, and twisted with temperature change, increased load, and lateral shift during the entire process between the suspension of the main cables and roof and ceiling construction (to be described later) *[fig.3-33, 3-34]*. The latter—the spherical band—is a component connecting the suspended steel beams and the main cables with a pin joint. More precisely, it is a spherical universal joint installed to allow omnidirectional rotation to prevent application of moments at the edges of the suspended steel beams caused by changes in the temperature, the roof's load, and the ropes in

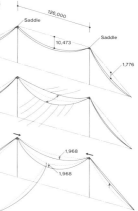

[fig.3-33] Irregularities in the main cables during installation strong winds [fig.3-35].[8]

[fig.3-34] Principle functions of the saddles: final positions, movement in tandem, omnidirectional rotation

While casting may produce iron products in diverse shapes, the process may also introduce gas porosity. Therefore castings used in the construction of the 1st gymnasium underwent strict inspec-

[fig.3-35] Spherical universal joint

tions (that of cast surfaces and dyeing methods, magnetic particle inspections, ultrasonic inspections, and drilling tests). Though the saddle's conical, complicated shape with constriction made it difficult to subject it to thorough inspection, it was considered to be sufficiently strong. Molybdenum disulfide was used as a lubricant to reduce the saddle's friction.

In addition, a wind tunnel experiment was performed to examine the effects of wind on the 1st gymnasium. It was confirmed that the wind load caused an uplifting force to the roof causing it to vibrate vertically. While the expected deformation was small (only 1/1300–1/650 of the span), vibration control dampers were planned for and installed between the main cables and towers underneath the monitor roof to serve as a safety measure for strong winds. This was despite the fact that equipping buildings with vibration control dampers was extremely rare at the time and that Negishi himself had utterly no experience employing these devices.

## 5. Suspension of the Cables
(December 10, 1963–January 10, 1964)

The steel framework beneath the saddle was installed before the process of pouring concrete for the towers was completed. Since this placement of the steel framework virtually determines the position of the main cables', the process was carried out with utmost care. The ropes for the main cables were suspended in the following steps: 1, carrier ropes were hung from gate-like towers 11m tall, built atop the main towers; 2, a rope reel was placed by the anchor block nearest to Harajuku, and the ropes were winched to the top of the tower on the Harajuku side; 3, ropes were reattached to carrier ropes placed between the towers and sent from the Harajuku side tower to the Shibuya side tower; 4, ropes were reattached to carrier ropes between the Shibuya side tower and anchor block on the Shibuya side and winched down from the top of the tower; and 5, both ends of the ropes were set into the sockets at the Harajuku- and Shibuya-side anchor blocks and their lengths were adjusted using horseshoe shims.[9]

The rope positions (lengths) were determined by the degree of sagging at the center and backstay at 20°C with no tension applied. However, the temperature at the core of the ropes could not be measured during daytime or right after sundown due to radiant heat and air temperatures, and thus measurements were conducted in the dead of night when there was no wind and little effect of heat. Because everything relied on the positioning of the first rope, the process took two or three days.

Once the first rope was set, it was assumed the bottom most position, where the following ropes were placed on top, layer by layer, working upward to form the shape of a circle. Three or four ropes (less than one level) were set during the day and adjusted at night. The rule of thumb for the installation of multiple ropes was: "neither touching nor far apart." But as the number of ropes increased to four or more levels, the ropes that had been nice an orderly placed at night would become distorted and disordered with upper ropes protruding the lower ropes due to expansion from uneven heating from radiant heat, even on overcast days. As the rope temperature stabilized at night, so too did their order [fig.3-36]. After trial and error through icy nights, 30m aboveground in flying scaffolds, the A and B ropes were suspended and gathered at 4.5m intervals with spherical and restraining bands. The ropes were first gathered at the halfway point, then again in quarters and eighths, thereby spacing out irregularities between the ropes and successfully suspending the two main cables.

Thereafter, using anchors installed near the upper columns on the edge of the RC gymnasium stand base, a single main cable

was pulled laterally by 21 ropes at once to its predetermined position. Then the monitor roof truss was installed between the two main cables, effectively fixing its shape *[fig.3-37–39]*. In fact, the installation of this monitor roof truss had been thought to be the most dangerous process on this construction site.[10] Assembled directly below the main cables in the pool, the truss was raised by carrier ropes and posi-

[fig.3-36] Suspending the main cables

[fig.3-37] *Preparing to spread the main cables laterally*

[fig.3-38] *Laterally spreading the main cables, installing the monitor roof*

[fig.3-39] *Preparing to install suspension beams while installing the monitor roof*

tioned perpendicular to the ground so that its ends could be pin-jointed with spherical bands to the main cables. The construction process was extremely unstable such that it was only after the purlins were installed that stability of the structure was recovered.

## 6. Change from Suspension Ropes to Suspension Beams and Their Installation

As aforementioned, the roofs structural support in the direction perpendicular to the main cables (side span) was the hanging net (employing suspension ropes) when construction first began, and stiffening ribs (long I-beams) were to be installed over the hanging net (suspension ropes) to provide rigidity. Many people on site pointed out the difficulty in producing these details. An ideal suspended roof has a surface in which the curvature changes continuously and is doubly curved with opposite curvature for the hanging net and restraining net components which both carry tensile forces.[11] Regarding the special boundary conditions of the 1st gymnasium (the three-dimensional gymnasium base and towers piercing the sky), experimental methods had already revealed the inability to shape the ideal curved roof with a combination of a hanging net and restraining net. It was here that Kawaguchi proposed replacing the hanging net and stiffening ribs with suspended steel members, which was adopted.

Further, structural calculations conducted earlier estimated a 2m increase in the sag in the main cables at the center between the erection of the monitor roof and completion of the roof construction. While the hanging net (suspension ropes) could connect the main cables and the edge of the gymnasium stand base and elongate elastically in response to increased roof loads, suspended beams were relatively fixed in shape and length, and it was revealed that they would be approximately 24cm short for the task. It was then decided to insert pin-joints *[fig.3-40–42]* at the middle of the beams, where there was zero bending moment. By doing so, they would initially connect the gymnasium stand base and main cables via a discontinuous curve and later, as roof construction progressed, produce a continuous curved roof. Put another way, Kawaguchi proposed a roof structure incorporating large-scale transformation (a semi-rigid roof structure), rather than steel members that would be suspended rigidly along the shape of the completed roof.

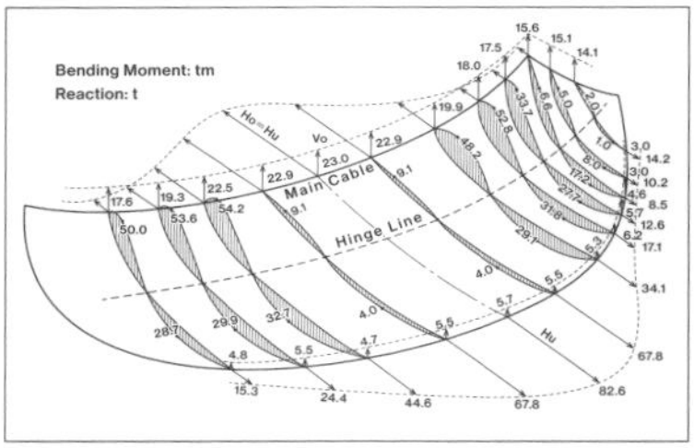

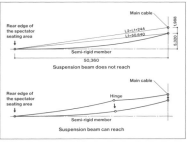

*[fig.3-40] The 1st gymnasium bending moment diagram*

*[fig.3-41] The main cable changes shape when hinges are installed on the suspension beam, allowing the suspension materials to reach the cable*

Next, a circular hole would be opened at the center of each steel beam's depth, through which restraining ropes would pass. Since the restraining ropes run perpendicular to the beams, their relative axial movement (translation) could result in lateral bending of the suspended steel beams.

Therefore, they were fixed with clamps to the beams in a way so that they could only rotate axially.

Regarding the production of the suspended steel members, the beams were up to 50m long and manufactured at a factory in two to seven parts. These were hauled to the site, raised with a tower crane, joined together on the pipe scaffolding, and welded after the joints had been subjected to rigorous inspection. It was feared at the time that the

varying manufacturing lengths of the beams would lead to noticeable uneven sagging and a non-smooth curved steel sheeted roof. Deviations from prescribed measurements were therefore limited to 2mm for one manufac-

[fig.3-42] Connecting the main cable and suspension beams

tured piece and 20mm for the entire steel beam length, and under such regulations the plate flanges and web stiffeners were welded by continuous fillet welding.

## 7. Installation of Purlins, Roofing Tomrex, and Ceiling Panels

Purlins (C channels) were installed once the suspended steel members were set. As the purlins are joined with bolts to the purlin supports attached to the suspended steel beams, the weight of the entire roof increases, leading to gradual deformation of the suspended steel beams. The bolt holes connecting the purlins were enlarged to accommodate this deformation, and one span in every two to three spans was void of purlins to allow for change in the curved roof's shape.[12]

4.5mm thick steel sheet roofing was then installed, with space allocated along the suspended steel members to accommodate deformation due to temperature changes. Further, roofing sheets were welded together on all four sides and the space allocated to accommodate temperature deformation was covered by battens welded on top. But still many difficulties arose, including dents caused by the crew walking on the roof during construction, and locations where rainwater puddled *[fig.3-43]*.[13]

With the roofing installed and restraining net (ropes) placed, the three-sided posts on the lower part of the gymnasium stand base were cautiously removed. Asbestos (Tomrex) was sprayed on the underside of the roof for

*[fig.3-43] Steel roofing sheets being installed on the suspension beams*

[fig.3-44] *Diving board, 1st gymnasium interior*

[fig.3-45] Interior construction,
1st gymnasium

[fig.3-46] Interior construction,
1st gymnasium

insulation and condensation prevention. In the initial design specification, the underside of the roof was to be finished with 2mm thick asphalt, but with the roofing sheets reaching 80°C in the summer and below freezing in the winter, the application of asphalt became impractical, let alone with a 2mm thickness. The finish was therefore changed to Tomrex. Even Tomrex proved difficult to spray uniformly upon the complex shape of the underside of the roof, leading to inadequate application.

The ceiling panels were installed after applying Tomrex; the number of panels totaled at 3,600, were composed of five types of panels excluding corners, with 2,500 of them manufactured in the factory and the rest on site. According to calculations, four workers per team would install 30 panels a day, but the 600 corner panel dimensions couldn't be determined until the panels had been installed to the edges, and so in the midsummer heat, workers climbed up and down the 30-meter-high scaffolding innumerable times. After the scaffolding was removed, the pool was finished, followed by adjustment of the facilities equipment, and the building was turned over in late August [fig.3-44–46].

1   Kaichi Negishi, "Kokuritsu okunai kyogi-jo no seko (1) [National Indoor Stadium Construction (1)]," Kenchikukai [Architectural World], April 1965, *55*.

2   Ministry of Construction Kanto Regional Development Bureau, "II kui uchi koji, sumi-dashi [II Pile Driving Work, Marking]," Kokuritsu okunai sogo kyogijo seko kiroku [National Indoor Stadium Construction Records], 1964, *18*.

3   Kaichi Negishi, "Kokuritsu okunai kyogi-jo no seko (1): 2 Kui koji to kiso [National Indoor Stadium Construction (1): 2 Piling and Foundation]," Kenchikukai [Architectural World], April 1965, *63*.

4   Ministry of Construction, "IV Katawaku koji: 5 Shihoko [IV Formwork: 5 Shoring]," Kokuritsu okunai sogo kyogijo seko kiroku [National Indoor Stadium Construction Records], 1964, *74*.

5   Kaichi Negishi, "Kokuritsu okunai kyogi-jo no seko (2): 5 Katawaku [National Indoor Stadium Construction (2): 5 Formwork]," Kenchikukai [Architectural World], May 1965, *65*.

6   Ministry of Construction, "VI Dai-1 taiikukan tsuri yane: 3 Zairyo no shiyo, kensa [VI The Suspended Roof of the 1st Gymnasium: 3 Use and Inspection of Materials]," Kokuritsu okunai sogo kyogijo seko kiroku [National Indoor Stadium Construction Records], 1964, *93*.

7   Kaichi Negishi, "Kokuritsu okunai kyogi-jo no seko (3): 9 Waiya ropu no seisaku [National Indoor Stadium Construction (3): 9 Manufacture of Wire Ropes]," Kenchikukai [Architectural World], June 1965, *50-51*.

8   Kaichi Negishi, "Kokuritsu okunai kyogi-jo no seko (4): 10 Chutetsu-hin no seisaku [National Indoor Stadium Construction (4): 10 Production of Cast Iron Materials]," Kenchikukai [Architectural World], July 1965, *27*.

9   Ministry of Construction, "VI Dai-1 taiikukan tsuri yane: 4 Seko [VI The Suspended Roof of the 1st Gymnasium: 4 Construction]," Kokuritsu okunai sogo kyogijo seko kiroku [National Indoor Stadium Construction Records], 1964, *97*.

10  Negishi, "Kokuritsu okunai kyogi-jo no seko (6): 15 Koshi-yane torasu no seko [National Indoor Stadium Construction (5): 15 Construction of the Monitor Roof Truss]," Kenchikukai [Architectural World], September 1965, *69*.

11  Mamoru Kawaguchi, "Yoyogi kyogijo dai-ichi taiikukan no kozo sekkei: Muttsu no mondai to kaiketsu keii [The Structural Design of Yoyogi National Gymnasium's 1st Gymnasium: Six Hurdles and Solutions]," Tange Kenzo wo kataru [On Tange Kenzo], Tokyo: Kajima Shuppankai, 2013, *140-145*.

12  Ministry of Construction, "VI Dai-ichi taiikukan tsuri yane: 4

Seko [VI The Suspended Roof of the 1st Gymnasium: 4 Construction],"
Kokuritsu okunai sogo kyogijo seko kiroku [National Indoor Stadium Construction Records], 1964, *101*.

13  Kaichi Negishi, "Kokuritsu okunai kyogi-jo no seko (6): 17 Yane teppan-bari [National Indoor Stadium Construction (6): 17 Iron Sheet Roofing]," Kenchikukai [Architectural World], August 1965, *71*.

# 4

# Yoyogi National Gymnasium after the 1964 Tokyo Olympics

# 4-1
## 1964–1973:
## Rapid Economic Growth

The Yoyogi National Gymnasium was built as a swimming and badminton venue for the 1964 Tokyo Olympics. Article 1 of the National Stadium Act indicates Yoyogi National Gymnasium's mission after the Olympics: to appropriately and efficiently operate the athletic facilities as well as to promote the spread of physical education and contribute to the healthy development of the people's minds and bodies. Here, physical education has a broad definition including physical education, sports, physical recreation, and so on. Further, Yoyogi National Gymnasium's operation policy was composed of the following three activities: first, its use as a venue for international and national sports competitions or similar events; second, its business as a facility open to the public; and third, its use in fostering and encouraging independent businesses and community sports to promote and spread national sports.[1]

Regarding the first, the facility's use for group activities, Yoyogi National Gymnasium hosted various national competitions annually, including national swimming championships (1966–) and the All-Japan Ice Hockey Championships (1968–) at the 1st Gymnasium and the All-Japan Intercollegiate Basketball Championships (1964–) at the 2nd Gymnasium. Yoyogi National Gymnasium was therefore expected to be maintained at the highest level of standards fitting for a venue hosting first-rate international competitions [fig.4-1, 4-2].[2]

[fig.4-1]  America's swimming team won the gold medal in women's 400m medley (Oct. 18, 1964)

As for the second, the facility's use for individuals, Yoyogi National Gymnasium began operating the 1st Gymnasium's ice skating rink and the swimming pool shortly after the Olympics, and adopted a policy for public use with the slogan "Providing facilities for anyone, anytime" [fig.4-3].[3] Construction on a dedicated kids' pool began in an area west of the 1st Gymnasium in May 1965. Approximately 1,000 children were invited on opening day August 5 [fig.4-4].[4]

[fig.4-2] Basketball game, America vs Peru (Oct. 13, 1964)

And as for the third, the facility's promotional business activities, "in the hopes of popularizing sports as an everyday affair," [5] Yoyogi National Gymnasium responded to the public's growing interest in sports by conducting various athletic programs from 1967 onward.[6] At the time, women's athletic programs and swimming classes were particularly popular, and the number of applicants far exceeded the capacity.

[fig.4-3] The 1st gymnasium as an ice skating rink

One of the limitations of Yoyogi National Gymnasium's athletic programs was that at-

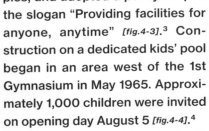

tendees were largely limited to local residents.
In an era the nationwide spread of sports, the
gymnasium planned and
implemented projects
aimed at the goal, "in
pursuit of a sustainable
model for athletic facil-
ities." [7] The reason being that despite the con-
siderable investment of
taxpayers' money in the
construction of national
facilities including those
from the Olympics, their

[fig.4-4] Environs: the kids' pool opens

use is limited after the end of the sports event.
Yoyogi National Gymnasium therefore initiat-
ed a variety of athletic programs aimed at test-
ing and researching strategies for efficient use
by local residents [fig.4-5].

Together with such promotional activities,
club rooms (training room,
lounge, etc.) were added
near the pool and ice
skating rink entrances,
providing indoor envi-
ronments where ath-
letes and coaches as
well as parents and
guardians could freely
interact.[8]

[fig.4-5] Women's athletic program held
in the environs and 2nd gymnasium

# 4-2

## 1973–1982:
## Oil Crisis and Aftermath

In October 1973, the Fourth Arab–Israeli War triggered a sharp increase in oil prices in Japan. As a result, Yoyogi National Gymnasium's heating system was shut down and its lighting reduced, which affected the number of ice skating rink and pool users as well as its earnings *[fig.4-6, 4-7]*.[9] Later, in response to soaring domestic prices, the facility raised its usage fees and sought to host events at the 1st Gymnasium.

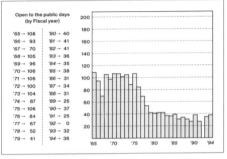

Open to the public days
(by Fiscal year)

| | | | |
|---|---|---|---|
| '65 → 108 | | '80 → 40 | |
| '66 → 93 | | '81 → 41 | |
| '67 → 70 | | '82 → 41 | |
| '68 → 105 | | '83 → 36 | |
| '69 → 96 | | '84 → 35 | |
| '70 → 106 | | '85 → 38 | |
| '71 → 106 | | '86 → 31 | |
| '72 → 100 | | '87 → 34 | |
| '73 → 104 | | '88 → 31 | |
| '74 → 87 | | '89 → 25 | |
| '75 → 106 | | '90 → 37 | |
| '76 → 84 | | '91 → 25 | |
| '77 → 67 | | '92 → 0 | |
| '78 → 52 | | '93 → 32 | |
| '79 → 41 | | '94 → 36 | |

*[fig.4-6] Public use of the 1st gymnasium pool, by fiscal year (1965-1994)*

With regard to the former, fees were increased on average by 30 percent in October 1974. Though Yoyogi National Gymnasium was a national facility, meaning the buildings' construction fees

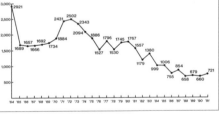

*[fig.4-7] Public use of the 1st gymnasium ice skating rink, by fiscal year*

had been shouldered entirely by the government, the national treasury did not entirely finance operational costs. Thus, the ideal was for the facility to operate independently as a business and it was required to draw closer to the ideal. "The idea that the participation in sports should cost nothing has widely spread through Japan since the Meiji Era, and to our detriment, this idea of free being best has not been rid of,"[10] points out a facility operator, who asks for public understanding on the increase in fees by arguing that the financial burdens placed on the beneficiaries would eventually contribute to the promotion of sports.

Regarding the latter, a policy was announced where sporting and other events would be hosted as often as possible once the pool or ice skating rink was converted to a gymnasium floor.[11] The first event to do so was the International Invitational Gymnastics Championships held in June 1976, for which a temporary floor was installed over the pool. And in November 1977, the 1st Gymnasium hosted the 2nd FIVB Volleyball Women's World Cup with a floor temporarily installed over the ice skating rink. Although the setup caused condensation due to the temperature differences above and below the floor, the tournament concluded successfully thanks to the efforts of numerous personnel. The tournament in fact allowed Yoyogi National Gymnasium to update its record of maximum number of visitors.

In late 1978, Yoyogi National Gymnasium facility managers enthusiastically debated management policies and printed them in the publication *National Stadium Monthly Magazine*. There are four important items among them: government subsidies, the posting of advertisement, alternative uses of the facility, and use of the environs.[12]

Concerning the first (that is, government subsidies), the facility as a whole was under the management of the national fiscal plan, and increased revenue did not entitle the facility to allocate spending at their own discretion. Facility operators then faced the dilemma of being unable to invest the revenue earned from planned business activities to increase the quality of service. With respect to the second item (advertising), although the placement of advertisements touched on the delicate issue between pro and amateur sports and was ultimately considered to be part of the facility's commercial activities, the National Stadium Advertising Placement Standards were established and enforced,[13] and then announced in March 1978. As for the third item, additional uses of the facility outside those intended were deemed consistent with the principles behind the facility itself. While prioritizing the facilities use as a venue for various international athletic tournaments, increasing operating rates for the 1st and 2nd Gymnasium would allow amateur athletes to use the facilities at lower prices. And regarding the fourth item, use of the environs[13] was suggested by the manager of the facilities, since its use for the kids' pool only two months per year during the summer was uneconomical.

# 4-3

## 1982–1992:
## Financial Reconstruction
## without Tax Increases and Holding of
## International Sports Fairs

### 1. Cultural Events Held at the 1st Gymnasium

To address declining tax revenue and enormous budget deficits following the oil crisis,
the government of Japan launched the Second Provisional Commission for Administrative Reform in 1981. The commission discussed privatization of Japanese National
Railways, Nippon Telegraph and Telephone
Corporation, and Japan Tobacco and Salt
Public Corporation to reconstruct the economy without raising taxes. As a result, in 1983,
a Cabinet decision integrated the Japan Society of School Health and the National Stadium,
which operated the Yoyogi National Gymnasium, and in 1984 the Second Provisional Commission for Administrative Reform report recommended the increased use of state-owned
facilities.

In response to the report, the Yoyogi National Gymnasium complied by aiming to increase facility usage while promoting the
popularization of sports, therefore shifting to
management-oriented facility operation. As
part of these endeavors, the National Stadium
and School Health Center of Japan Act was

enacted in December 1985, declaring physical education facilities to be opened to the general public (use in cultural events) provided that business operations not be hindered. Although this permission came with a caveat, Yoyogi National Gymnasium could now host cultural events [fig.4-8].[14]

## 2. The World Sports Fair
That Employed a Transmedia Franchise

Following the establishment and enforcement of the National Stadium Advertising Placement Standards in 1977, Yoyogi National Gymnasium revised its advertising fees and abolished the limit on the number of allowable postings. Trends in business and advertising agencies are thought to have influenced these changes.[15] For example, Yoyogi National Gymnasium hosted the annual World Sports Fair (sponsored by Japan Sport Association, Fuji Television Network, Sankei Shimbun, and others) from 1983 to 1992. In organizing this event, sponsors pointed out the following four aspects of the historical background. First, with the growth of an aging population and an increase in leisure time, Japan had entered an era wherein sports was something to be enjoyed across all age groups. Second, the number of people playing sports with a purpose for fashion, communication with others, or recreation had increased. Third, mass media had played a large role in popularizing interest in and knowl-

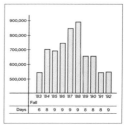

[fig.4-8] Total number of visitors to World Sports Fair

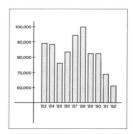

[fig.4-9] Average number of visitors to World Sports Fair per day

edge and information about sports by increasing and diversifying sporting events and televising sports programs. Fourth, sports- and health-related industries were rapidly developing.

Based on the recognition of such factors, the 1st Gymnasium, 2nd Gymnasium, and special outdoor stage hosted various organized events as well as nationwide television and radio broadcasts, primarily for sporting events and music programs. The number of spectators over a six-day period in 1983 totaled at 540,000,[16] and with Yoyogi National Gymnasium as the stage, the citywide event employed a transmedia franchise of newspapers, television, and radio.

The World Sports Fair was held for 10 years, its total number of spectators rising to approximately 6.3 million, and from 1987 onward, facilities in Yoyogi National Gymnasium's vicinity simultaneously held various sporting events. The number of visitors gradually decreased beginning in 1989, however, and the fair came to a close in 1992 [fig.4-8–10].

[fig.4-10] 18th Camping Car & RV Show

## 4-4

## 1992–2001:
## Expansion and Renovation of Yoyogi National Gymnasium to Increase the Operating Rate

### 1. Demolition of the Kids' Pool and Redefining Green Space

In 1993, the kids' pool built at the northwestern part of the Yoyogi National Gymnasium was demolished, and attempts to improve the environs' operating rate began. Further, the "Guidelines for Use of Yoyogi National Gymnasium West Plaza (Tentative Name)" were established and a simple outdoor athletic facility was constructed at the kids' pool site.

In April 1995, the regulations on the use of the National Stadium were partially revised and rental price standards for the gymnasium environs were introduced in order to promote its use and meet the needs of its users. The revisions were composed of four tasks, the first of which was to name the various areas of the gymnasium environs. Second, establish fees for use of the environs. Third, establish advertising standards for the environs. And fourth, establish standards for parking fees for the environs.

Regarding the first task of naming, the site of the old kids' pool and surrounding area was named Olympic Plaza. What had formerly been called the Bus Terminal at the southwestern part of the site was named Shibuya Plaza due to its location near Shibuya. The area had literally served as a terminal, as the location where buses transporting visitors to Yoyogi National Gymnasium parked, since the gymanisum was one of the tourist attractions on the Hato Bus Tokyo sightseeing course. The area lost its purpose as a bus terminal when Yoyogi National Gymnasium was taken off the Hato Bus sightseeing course in 1995. Meanwhile, Harajuku Exit Plaza was for geographical reasons named Harajuku Plaza *[fig.4-11]*.[17]

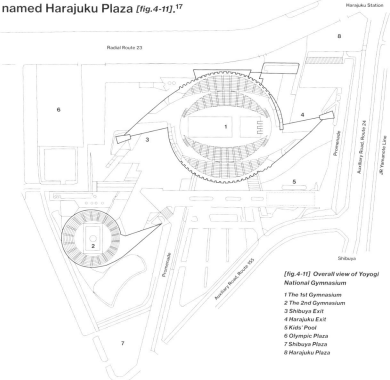

*[fig.4-11] Overall view of Yoyogi National Gymnasium*

*1 The 1st Gymnasium*
*2 The 2nd Gymnasium*
*3 Shibuya Exit*
*4 Harajuku Exit*
*5 Kids' Pool*
*6 Olympic Plaza*
*7 Shibuya Plaza*
*8 Harajuku Plaza*

## 2. Expansion and Renovation of the 1st Gymnasium and Free Admission for the Ice Skating Rink

Complying with the final report of the Second Provisional Commission for Administrative Reform, the 1st Gymnasium underwent distinctive renovations as well. First, to further promote use of the gymnasium floor, the northern lobby underwent construction for expansion as well as to prevent land subsidence. More specifically, starting in 1992, space allotted for existing systems (that is, the pool filtration equipment) had been reduced to secure space for doorways, slopes, and performer waiting rooms. Second, the 1st Gymnasium's air conditioning system, which had been an issue of concern since the completion of construction, was finally realized in the year 2000. Further, the 1st Gymnasium pool was closed to the public in 1997 and the diving platform was removed in April 2002.[18]

As for the ice skating rink in the 1st Gymnasium, the regular customers at the year 2000 primarily consisted of the Tokyo Olympics generation (middle-aged and older), and the departure from skating was expected to accelerate. For this reason, January 6, 2001 was set as an admission free day for Yoyogi National Gymnasium. Promotion of alternative uses for the facility since the 1980s had resulted in the decline of the ice skating rink's popularity, and facility operators expressed concern over the 1st Gymnasium's primary image as a sporting event and concert venue. They came to the conclusion that the mass media (broadcasts and newspaper and other publications) circulating information on its use as a venue for sporting events and concerts may have weakened the image of the gymnasium's function as an ice skating rink.[19]

# 4-5
## 2001 and Beyond: Becoming an Independent Administrative Institution

### 1. Setting of a Target Operating Rate, Reduction of Personnel, and Outsourcing as an Independent Administrative Institution

In 2001, the Cabinet approved the Reorganization and Rationalization Plan of Special Public Institutions, and it was decided that the National Stadium and School Health Center of Japan managing Yoyogi National Gymnasium would become an Independent Administrative Institution. The Japan Sport Council (the Independent Administrative Institution in question) was established on October 1, 2003.

The Japan Sport Council was positioned as a central, specialized institution to promote sports and plan the maintenance and advancement of children's and students' health in Japan. Further, Yoyogi National Gymnasium's target days of operation was set, and while continuing to be used as a facility for national and international sporting events, the facility operators also engaged in business activities to promote the gymnasium's use as a venue for concerts, cultural events, and the like to secure revenue and to effectively use the facility. Until then, Yoyogi National Gymnasium's usage statistics, reflecting the prioritization of athletic activities of organizations, the general population, and promotional activities in the given order, had been disclosed in detail. However, since becoming an independent administrative institution, the facility operators disclosed only limited data, such as target versus actual days of operation and total versus paying visitors.

## 2. Improvement of the Facility for the Tokyo 2020 Olympics

On September 7, 2013, the IOC, at their 125th meeting in Buenos Aires, decided to host the 2020 Olympic and Paralympic Games in Tokyo. Yoyogi National Gymnasium was to host the handball competitions for the Olympics and the wheelchair rugby competitions for the Paralympics. The gymnasium is consequently undergoing large-scale repairs.

[fig.4-13] Recent image of Yoyogi
National Gymnasium (2011)

1   "Kokuritsu kyogijo: Shisetsu ippan riyo kitei no kaisei ni atatte [On the Revision of the National Stadium's General Use Regulations]," Gekkan kokuritsu kyogijo [National Stadium Monthly Magazine], October 1974, 6.

2   Tomonari Kaneda, "Kokuritsu kyogijo ni okeru supotsu no fukyu jigyo [Popularization of Sports at the National Stadium]," Gekkan kokuritsu kyogijo [National Stadium Monthly Magazine], October 1976, 2.

3   Mikisuke Masuda, "Sakunendo (Showa 45-nendo) kokuritsu kyogijo [Last Year (1970) National Stadium]," Gekkan kokuritsu kyogijo [National Stadium Monthly Magazine], April 1971, 2.

4   Kokuritsu kyogijo 50-nen no ayumi [National Stadium: A 50-Year Journey], ed. Kokuritsu kyogijo 50-nen-shi henshu iinkai-hen [National Stadium 50-Year History Editorial Committee Edition] (Tokyo: Japan Sport Council, 2012), 39.

5   "Showa 46-nendo kokuritsu kyogijo riyo jokyo ni tsuite [Regarding National Stadium Use in FY 1971]," editorial department, Gekkan kokuritsu kyogijo [National Stadium Monthly Magazine], April 1972, 5.

6   Kokuritsu kyogijo 50-nen no ayumi [National Stadium: A 50-Year Journey], ed. Kokuritsu kyogijo 50-nen-shi henshu iinkai-hen [National Stadium 50-Year History Editorial Committee Edition] (Tokyo: Japan Sport Council, 2012), 44.

7   Tomonari Kaneda, "Kokuritsu kyogijo ni okeru supotsu no fukyu jigyo [Popularization of Sports at the National Stadium]," Gekkan kokuritsu kyogijo [National Stadium Monthly Magazine], October 1976, 3.

8   Kokuritsu kyogijo 50-nen no ayumi [National Stadium: A 50-Year Journey], ed. Kokuritsu kyogijo 50-nen-shi henshu iinkai-hen [National Stadium 50-Year History Editorial Committee Edition] (Tokyo: Japan Sport Council, 2012), 52.

9   "Showa 48-nendo kokuritsu kyogijo riyo jokyo [National Stadium Use in FY 1973]," editorial department, Gekkan kokuritsu kyogijo [National Stadium Monthly Magazine], April 1974, 6.

10  "Kokuritsu kyogijo: Shisetsu ippan riyo kitei no kaisei ni atatte [On the Revision of the National Stadium's General Use Regulations]," Gekkan kokuritsu kyogijo [National Stadium Monthly Magazine], October 1974, 7.

11  Ikuharu Sugawa, "Yoyogi kyogijo dai-ichi taiikukan furoa to shite no riyou no henkan [Transition to Use of Yoyogi National Gymnasium's 1st Gymnasium with a Gym Floor]," Gekkan kokuritsu kyogijo [National Stadium Monthly Magazine], September 1982, 2-5.

12  Eiichi Yamaguchi et. al., "Zadan-kai: Kokuritsu kyogijo no un'ei wo megutte [Roundtable: On the Management of the National Stadium]," Gekkan kokuritsu kyogijo [National Stadium Monthly Magazine], December 1978, 5–11.

13  Hisashi Igarashi and Tatsuo Akatani, "Yoyogi enchi no riyo ripoto: megumareta kankyo ikashi hiroba saiji wa nennen zoka [Report on Use of Yoyogi Grounds: Events Leveraging Bountiful Environment Increasing Annually]," Gekkan kokuritsu kyogijo [National Stadium Monthly Magazine], July 1995, 4.

14  Ibid., 2.

15  Ibid., 4.

16  "Supotsu no banpaku: Kokusai supotsu fea '83 aki, seikyo no uchi ni shuryo [Sports Expo: '83 Fall International Sports Fair Ends in Success]," second business department section, Gekkan kokuritsu kyogijo [National Stadium Monthly Magazine], October 1983, 10–11.

17  Hisashi Igarashi and Tatsuo Akatani, "Yoyogi enchi no riyo ripoto: megumareta kankyo ikashi hiroba saiji wa nennen zoka [Report on Use of Yoyogi Grounds: Events Leveraging Bountiful Environment Increasing Annually]," Gekkan kokuritsu kyogijo [National Stadium Monthly Magazine], July 1995, 3.

18  "Kohi bureiku: Kyodaina kosakubutsu ga shikai kara kieru [Coffee Break: Giant Structure Disappears from Sight],"Gekkan kokuritsu kyogijo [National Stadium Monthly Magazine], June 2002, 11.

19  Shogo Seki , "Shinki kakutoku to ripita kakuho de mokuhyo wo ohaba ni uwamawaru zennen-hi 68%-zo Yoyogi kyogijo suketojo (1/6–2/13) no shukyaku sakusen [Yoyogi National Gymnasium Ice Skating Rink (Jan. 6–Feb. 13) Strategy to Attract Customers, Greatly Exceeds Target, Up 68 Percent from Last Year with New Clients and Repeating Customers]," Gekkan kokuritsu kyogijo [National Stadium Monthly Magazine], April 2001, 4–5.

# Conclusion

The five characteristics of Kenzo Tange's urban and architectural design, introduced in Chapter 1, all present themselves integrated to the highest degree in Yoyogi National Gymnasium, one of the pinnacles of Tange's work.

The first, regarding modernity and tradition, can be seen in the implementation of the suspended roof structure. The suspended roof is typically used to express lightness like that of a circus tent as can be seen in the Munich Olympic Stadium, which uses a transparent cable net structure. In comparison, Yoyogi National Gymnasium's suspended roof uses heavy iron sheets reminiscent of the heavily tiled temple roofs found in Asia, combining tradition with state-of-the -art technology.

The second, regarding war and peace, the site Yoyogi has a history of usage as an army parade ground and thereafter as a base occupied by GHQ (Washington Heights), and still later as a venue for the Olympic Games, a festival celebrating peace. In this regard, the land of Yoyogi is a place in which the 20th century history of Japan has been diligently engraved, and Tange designed the stadium so athletes from around the world could come together, compete, and celebrate each other's accomplishments.

The third, regarding postwar democracy and government buildings of which the main topic is the organic integration between the urban and architectural core, Tange deals with and integrates the various activities of the widely demographically varying people, such as the tens of thousands of spectators, tournament officials, athletes, and VIPs, by taking advantage of the difference in elevation within the site.

The fourth, regarding the endeavors to large span structures, can be seen in Tange's employment of a suspended roof structure to cloak the 110m-diameter ring of Yoyogi National Gymnasium. This selection is based on his bitter experiences with problematic defects arising from flawed construction in concrete shell roof structures of increasing sizes that he implemented in his designs in the 1950s.

The fifth, regarding design during rapid economic growth, the gymnasium was planned with a near-futuristic design in a prime location between Shibuya and Harajuku Station, symbolizing Japan's postwar recovery and rapid economic growth to the world.

It is worth mentioning that half a century after construction, the buildings still maintain their beautiful silhouette and remain widely and frequently used as multipurpose facilities. In the preliminary drawings, Tange indicated his intention to hint the excitement of sports in an urban landscape and to form architecture with a beautiful appearance and striking layout that would affirm to the expectations that the gathering spectators have towards the tournaments held within the facility. It can be said that even now the buildings have inherited this philosophy in its design.

Further, into the 2000s, the use as a gymnasium rather than as a swimming pool was prioritized in the 1st Gymnasium, and while adapting to societal needs, this transition also greatly contributed to extending the life of the facility.

# Afterword

In November 1965, one year after the 1964 Tokyo Summer Olympics  came to a close, Tange touches on the difference between abstraction and symbolism in his essay "Kukan to shocho [Space and Symbolism]." According to Tange, the former is the process of removing meaning, while the latter is the process of sublimating meaning into a concentrated form. He then discusses, as follows, the meaning of the Yoyogi National Gymnasium as a symbol in contemporary society:

*When designing the Olympic National Indoor Stadium, I was vaguely conscious of the psychological, emotional, and spiritual eloquence of the space. One might say it was a passage leading between the physical and metaphysical. It was hardly something so inflated as to be recognized as an answer to the question of "what is the symbol of the will of today", but it may have been a rudimentary approach to such an idea.*

*When the National Indoor Stadium was so fortunately awarded the Olympic Diploma of Merit by the IOC, President Brundage explained his reasoning in the following sentiment, that it might be said an architect's work was inspired by sports, and as evidenced by the many world records set there, the athletes found inspiration in the architecture itself. He went on to say this indoor stadium would deeply engrave itself in the memories not only for the citizens of Tokyo but also for those who visited it, and those who participated in or witnessed the games held there. That it would be clearly engraved in the memories of those who love beauty.*

*This was excessive praise for us. But I rather deeply felt it raised important ideas.*

*Among them pertains to the interaction of architectural spaces and the human spirit, not whether these buildings had succeeded or failed at it but rather the importance of the issue itself. Another is that I was taught to consider a mindset where architectural spaces worth remembering are vital places for cultivating human character.*

For a national event on the scale of the Tokyo Olympics, Tange brought to fruition a physical indoor stadium accommodating over ten thousand spectators while being keenly aware of the metaphysical eloquence required of such structures. Architect Ludwig Mies van der Rohe once pointed out in a 1924 lecture, "Architecture is the will of an epoch translated into space," and if taking the IOC president's compliments at face value, one might say the Yoyogi National

Gymnasium is a symbol of the will of today translated into physical space.

Additionally, Tange identifies two ideas in the IOC president's compliments (those being the importance of interaction between architectural space and the human spirit, and the importance of architectural spaces engraved in human memory for cultivating human character). Recalling the many sports competitions drawing athletes from across the nation and the globe, the splendid cultural festivals, and the national events held without interruption at Yoyogi National Gymnasium for half a century after the Olympic Games, one might indeed continuously affirm of the importance of interaction between architectural space and the human spirit, as well as the importance of an architectural space engraved in human memory for cultivating human character.

# Image Credits

Asahi Shimbun Photo Archives: *fig.2-1, 2-2, 4-2, 4-3*

Construction Engineering Research Institute,
"National Indoor Stadium Facilities Preliminary Design Guide,"
National Archives of Japan, March 20, 1962, 9–11: *fig.3-10~22*

Fumihiko Maki and Koji Kamiya ed.,
Tange Kenzo wo kataru [On Kenzo Tange],
Kajima Institute Publishing, 2013, 143: *fig.3-41*

Gekkan kokuritsu kyogijo [National Stadium Monthly Magazine],
August 25, 1965: *fig.4-4*
Ibid., October 25, 1969: *fig.4-5*
Ibid., June 25, 1987: *fig.4-10*
Ibid., May 25, 1992: *fig.4-8, 4-9*
Ibid., January 25, 1993: *fig.4-7*
Ibid., February 25, 1995: *fig.4-6*
Ibid., July 25, 1995: *fig.4-12*

Japan Sport Council: *fig.4-11*

Kanto Regional Architectural Division, Maintenance Section,
Kokuritsu okunai sogo kyogijo seko kiroku
[Yoyogi National Gymnasium Construction Records], 1964: *fig.3-9, 3-31*

Kawaguchi & Engineers: *pp.9~24, fig.3-28, 3-35*

Kenchiku [Architecture], June 1965, 52: *fig.1-26*

Kenchiku bunka [The Architectural Culture],
February 1958, 48: *fig.1-25*
Ibid., January 1965, 86: *fig.3-5~8*
Ibid., January 1965, 91: *fig.3-40*
Ibid., January 1965, 100: *fig.3-33~34*
Ibid., January 1965, 112: *fig.3-24, 3-25*

Kenchiku zasshi [Journal of Architecture and Building Science],
December 1942: *fig.1-8*
Ibid., November 1949: *fig.1-9, 1-10*

Masakazu Koyama, Dependento hausu [Dependents Housing], Gijutsu Shiryo Kankokai, 1948: *fig.2-9, 2-10*

Masamitsu Nagashima: *fig.1-34*

Nikkan Sports: *fig.4-1*

Saikaku Toyokawa: *fig.1-13~16, 1-22, 1-27, 1-28, 1-33*

Shimizu Corporation, Photograph: *fig.3-1~4, 3-26, 3-27, 3-29, 3-30, 3-32, 3-36~39, 3-42~46*

Shinkenchiku [New Architecture], April 1967, 167: *fig.1-31, 1-32*

Taro Okamoto Museum of Art, Kawasaki City: *fig.1-18*

The Tokyo Institute for Municipal Reserch: *fig.2-3, 2-4*

Tokyo Metropolitan Archives, Uchida Library: *fig.2-6*

Toshi shiryo shusei II, dai 7-kan: Orinpikku to Tokyo [Tokyo History Collection II, Vol. 7: The Olympics and Tokyo], ed. Tokyo Metropolitan Archives, Tokyo Metropolitan Cultural Affairs Bureau, Tokyo Metropolitan Archives ed., 2018: *fig.2-11*

Toshio Suzuki, Olympic Road Map, Shintoshi, 1963.6, 6: *fig.2-12*

Tsuboi Yoshikatsu Structural Design Office: "National Indoor Stadium Structural Calculations, 1," Kawaguchi Kenichi Lab, Institute of Industrial Science, University of Tokyo, October 1962, 2: *fig.3-23*

Uchida Archives: *fig.1-2~7, 1-11, 1-12, 1-17, 1-19~21, 1-23, 1-24, 1-29, 1-30*

University of Tokyo Library B (Architecture): *fig.1-1*

1940 Summer Olympics in Tokyo Report, Tokyo City Hall, 1939: *fig.2-5, 2-7, 2-8*

## Saikaku Toyokawa

Architect and architectural historian. Born 1973 in Miyagi prefecture. Associate professor in the Department of Urban Environment Systems, Faculty of Engineering, Chiba University. Doctor of engineering, registered first-class architect. Studied at the Department of Architecture, Graduate School of Engineering, Tokyo University, and worked for Nihon Sekkei before assuming current post. Guest curator of the exhibition TANGE BY TANGE 1949–1959 (GALLERY·MA, 2015). Publications include Gunzō to shite no Tange Kenkyūshitsu (Ohmsha, 2012; AIJ Book Prize).

The publication of this book was
made possible, in part,
by World Monuments Fund through support
from American Express.

# Yoyogi National Gymnasium and KENZO TANGE

First published in Japan on March 10, 2021

Author: Saikaku Toyokawa

Publisher: Takeshi Ito

TOTO Publishing (TOTO LTD.)
TOTO Nogizaka Bldg., 2F
1-24-3 Minami-Aoyama, Minato-ku
Tokyo 107-0062, Japan
[Sales]     Telephone: +81-3-3402-7138
             Facsimile:   +81-3-3402-7187
[Editorial] Telephone: +81-3-3497-1010
URL: https://jp.toto.com/publishing

Book Designer: Yoshiaki Shioya

Translator: Fraze Craze Inc.
Supervisor of Translation: Tsuyoshi Koyama

Printer: AKATSUKI PRINTING INC

Printed in Japan
ISBN 978-4-88706-389-1